INNOKENTIJ ANNENSKIJ AND THE ACMEIST DOCTRINE

Janet G. Tucker

Slavica Publishers, Inc.

Slavica publishes a wide variety of textbooks and scholarly books on the languages, people, literatures, cultures, history, and folklore of the USSR and Eastern Europe. For a complete catalog of books and journals from Slavica, with prices and ordering information, write to:

Slavica Publishers, Inc.
PO Box 14388
Columbus, Ohio 43214

ISBN: 0-89357-164-4

323291

c

Printed in the United States of America.

Item	*Chapter*	*Page*

For Bill and Rob

CONTENTS

PREFACE

Innokentij Fedorovič Annenskij was one of the most elusive figures of Russian modernism. He shunned Symbolism, the major school of his time, although elements of Symbolist aesthetics can be detected in his work. His verse anticipates practically all the principal movements in Russian poetry in the first half of the twentieth century.[1]

Annenskij's pedagogical experience and aesthetic independence made him especially attractive for the Acmeists, a poetic group that eschewed the mystical and abstract excesses of the later Symbolists while simultaneously avoiding the radical experimentation of the Futurists. While the link between Annenskij and the Acmeists has been mentioned in passing, no critic has yet determined the reasons for and nature of the tie between them. This study will attempt to close that gap, touching on those facets of Annenskij's work most closely related to the Acmeists' literary doctrine, and focusing, through thematic categorization of Annenskij's poetry and an analysis of his poetic devices, on his aesthetic and philosophical affinities with the younger poets. A discussion of this connection will not only shed light on Annenskij and the Acmeists, but will define an entire period of Russian literature. It will further serve the purposes of this work to include an investigation of those points of the Acmeist doctrine embodied in three articles by its major theoreticians Nikolaj Gumilev, Sergej Gorodeckij, and Osip Mandel'štam. Additional light can be shed by an essay of the Symbolist poet Mixail Kuzmin, a precursor of the Acmeists. The poetry of the Acmeists should also be discussed in passing as a vital corollary to this work, a study intended to clarify the relationships among poetic schools in Russian literature at the beginning of this century and to analyze Annenskij's role in the literature of this period.

I would like to thank Professor Maurice Friedberg, Head of the Department of Slavic Languages and Literatures at the University of Illinois, for the initial idea that led to this study and for valuable suggestions that improved it immeasurably. I am especially indebted to Professor James J. Hudson, Dean of the Graduate School at the University of Arkansas and Professor of History, for his encouragement, assistance, and optimism, and to Michael O'Brien and James Briscoe for invaluable editorial comments and suggestions. Both Michael O'Brien and James Briscoe generously shared their computers and eased my task considerably. I am grateful to my husband William Tucker and son Robert Eliot Tucker for their helpful suggestions and patience in the face of my unremitting work, to my parents, Julius and Rose Fine, and to Gilbert and Anne Cour for their years of encouragement. I would also like to thank the late Carl Proffer and Ellendea Proffer, editors of *Russian Literature Triquarterly*, for permission to reprint the essay that constitutes Chapter Four of the present study, as well as the Interlibrary Loan Department at the Indiana University Library for their valuable assistance. Any mistakes and shortcomings are my own.

Transliteration from the Cyrillic

I have chosen to use Transliteration System III from J. Thomas Shaw's pamphlet, *The Transliteration of Modern Russian for English-Language Publications* (Madison: The University of Wisconsin Press, 1967).

Fayetteville, Arkansas

May, 1985

CHAPTER ONE

RUSSIAN MODERNISM:
ANNENSKIJ AND THE SYMBOLISTS

The various literary movements constituting modernism in Russia differed in their aesthetic values and world views, but they shared and were characterized by a common desire for change from established literary practices. The complexities of the three principal movements, Symbolism, Acmeism, and Futurism, are such that an awareness of the reasons for their revolts is vital to an understanding of the movements themselves.

One of the principal driving forces of modernism was its constant search for change and a desire to posit new parameters for placing the arts within the context of what must have been seen as an increasingly complex and incomprehensible environment. The realism dominating literature into the latter part of the nineteenth century came more and more to be seen as an unsatisfactory means of coping with whatever lay beneath superficial reality, particularly in the face of its possible fragmentation. The framework of society seemed to be disintegrating in fin-de-siècle Russia. The period prior to World War One and the Russian Revolution was a time of growing tension, when ominous changes beyond the control of the existing order threatened to occur and finally came to fruition throughout Europe, but especially in Russia.

The bankruptcy of the established system impelled artists to posit their own values as a substitute to fill the vacuum left by what had been lost. Because there was no longer an accepted, traditional way of apprehending reality or even of defining it, each of the three modernist groups put forth its own stipulations governing the relationship between art and whatever lay outside it, substituting thereby its own particular set of values.

The Symbolists were both drawn to and horrified by the approaching cataclysmic changes haunting fin-de-siècle Russia, and

they alternatively used art as either escape from that reality or as
a way of transcending it.   Revolution came to be seen as the
means whereby superficial existence could be erased or distorted
with the unknown, the abyss, taking its place.   The wind from
that engulfing emptiness blows through two apocalyptic
revolutionary Symbolist works central to the movement, Aleksandr
Blok's poem "The Twelve" and Andrej Belyj's novel *Petersburg*.
Each work deals with the destruction of the real protagonist,
Westernized Russia.

Symbolism sprang up in reaction to and protest against the
civic poetry that had dominated Russian verse in the 1870s and
1880s, a poetry preoccupied with the same motifs championed by
the civic critics of the nineteenth century.   The impact of this
civic orientation was sufficiently great for poetry to have ceased
functioning as independent lyrical expression by the late 1800s.   In
any but the most strictly formal sense, it was a period of prose,
not poetry, with prose in poetic guise continuing to dominate later
nineteenth-century Russian literature. This phenomenon produced a
situation that the Symbolists not only changed but even, to an
extent, exploited.   In their efforts to re-establish the independence
of verse, they called for its complete reassessment; they ended the
reign of prose and ushered in a period of poetic supercedence, but
it was poetry according their terms.[1]   They were so repelled by
their predecessors that they disavowed any attempt to reproduce
reality in art, and they were self-consciously aware that positing
new values at this time would assure them of a place in history.
The Symbolists experimented in verse techniques and asserted that
poetry should be musical and suggestive, not pictorial and specific.
The new conception of poetry they left to Russian literature
followed, in the main, the range of subjects and techniques of the
French Symbolists.[2]   For approximately fifteen years following its
sudden birth, Symbolism was itself to be the principal force in
Russian letters.

One facet of the Symbolist revolt against the civic poets was
a pointed retreat from realism.   Art came to be seen as a desirable
substitute for reality, particularly for the later Symbolists, and
reality became distorted.   Death and dreams assumed new
significance as a means of escape, realms in limbo between reality
and unreality.[3]   This was a role that was to be filled in the
physical world by revolution.   Revolution, dream, and death were
intricately linked as different aspects of the same phenomenon,

negative, destructive alternatives to reality. Art as replacement for
reality was regarded as a separate mode of experience, not merely
as the product of the creative imagination.[4]

With art no longer responsible to external stimulae, poetry
changed from a visually-oriented medium to one in which music
and the sounds of words predominated over meaning. Paul
Verlaine's tenet of the "musico-emotional expression of lyrical
moods" and Schopenhauer's theory of music as the "ideal and
absolute form of art" were especially appealing for the later
Symbolists.[5] Clarity lost ground to indefiniteness; form yielded to
formlessness.

Symbolism was not a monolithic movement, and the
Symbolists can be divided into two groups roughly along
chronological lines, with the older or first generation holding sway
in advance of the younger or second one. Both groups had their
gurus, Dmitrij Merežkovskij and Valerij Brjusov for the older poets
and Vjačeslav Ivanov and Andrej Belyj for the younger. The
revolts *qua* revolts characteristic of modernist movements
throughout Europe penetrated Symbolism itself, for the school was
too diverse both chronologically and in the number of its adherents
to endure long as a single movement. Symbolism echoed too the
rapid social changes and feeling of impending doom with which
Russian society of this period was imbued, and the older writers'
despair at living in what they considered a dying age gave way to
the younger poets' fascination with the dynamics of a revolution
whose distant echoes they were beginning to sense.

Such writers of the first generation as Brjusov, Fedor Sologub,
and Zinaida Gippius shared a desire to shock the reader, an
inclination that found expression in, for example, Sologub's and
Gippius' dabbling in verbal evil and perversion. These first writers
were acutely aware of being adherents of a new literary school, and
their earliest work was self-consciously separate from that of the
preceding civic generation.[6] One symptom of this independence
was a rejection of such traditional facets of Russian civic poetry as
an emphasis on visual images and a preoccupation with social
injustice. In short, it was a repudiation of realism, of the
limitations of Russian nationalism in favor of the new Western art,
although the later Symbolists would draw, once again, on their
Russian background. Because prose was identified with the status
quo, literary experimentation came to be associated with poetry,
specifically, with the new Symbolist poetry of the French, and it

was these latter writers who were the models for European
modernism in general and for the Russian Symbolists in particular.
In their retreat from the specificity of detail and image
characteristic of the civic poets, the early Symbolists were drawn to
Mallarmé's emphasis on suggestiveness and Verlaine's appeal for
vagueness.[7]

The Russian Symbolists shunned concrete images and
emphasized sound; the word or symbol functioned as an indicator
of a secret existence, and obscurity replaced distinct outlines.[8] A
marked increase in the use of abstract nouns and epithets and a
breakdown in the logical links between words led to irrationality
and obscurity.[9] Typically, the older Symbolist poet Konstantin
Bal'mont echoed his mentor Dmitrij Merežkovskij in considering
himself a non-realist, maintaining that "realists are always
observers, symbolists—always thinkers . . . ."[10] The Symbol was
an "expression of an entire complex of sensations, emotions, and
impressions of an subject"; it was transformed into a "hint of some
secret existence," and realms of "ideal nature" and of the "creative
dream" were revealed to the Symbolists in language by the word,
the "living link of sounds and meaning."[11]

The older Symbolists were influenced by their French
predecessors, but their younger counterparts looked instead to
German Romantic philosophy, specifically to Schelling, and to
Schopenhauer and Nietzsche, whose tragic perception of the
universe and belief that the human spirit contained extensive
possibilities for transcending the commonplace world were to be
reflected in the work of Blok and Belyj. The Russian mystical
philosopher Vladimir Solov'ev, who argued that the world
surrounding the poet was a lower stratum of existence and that art
served to separate beauty from coarse reality, was their mentor.[12]
Solov'ev's belief that there was a correspondence between earthly
existence and a pretersensual, "higher" reality had a great impact
on the younger poets.[13] His signal contribution both to Russian
philosophy and to later Russian Symbolism was his conception of
Divine Wisdom, or the Eternal Feminine, Sophia, a doctrine having
an enormous influence on the poetry of Aleksandr Blok, particularly
in the "Stixi o prekrasnoj dame" ("Verses about the Beautiful
Lady").[14] Blok would express his later disillusionment with Sophia
in his so-called "Gypsy" poetry. The higher, transcendent,
mystical realms of existence were embodied in Sophia, who made
that transcendent reality comprehensible and, to an extent, concrete

for the later Symbolists. Solov'ev's vital, albeit premature, contribution to Symbolism lay in his ability to distill the definite form of Sophia from the chaos of mysticism.

Attraction to the teachings of Vladimir Solov'ev was symptomatic not only of the later Symbolists' increased interest in mysticism, but also of a new swing away from Western European literature and the orientation of the first generation. Belyj maintained that Russian Symbolism was more deeply "grounded" than that of the French, since it was linked to national literature and poetry.[15] If the younger poets' basic tie was to Vladimir Solov'ev and the "Nietzchean" philosophy anticipated in the novels of Dostoevskij, than it is reasonable for French Symbolism to have been of only passing interest.[16]

The younger poets' rejection of the French writers is a facet of their rebellion against the older generation and a repudiation of the earlier view that the literary work was the focal point of the creative effort. Belyj, Blok, and Vjačeslav Ivanov were mystics who conceived of Symbolism as a new world view with poetry a religious rite and the poet a prophet.[17] The first generation's adherence to the French Symbolists' theory of correspondences, their use of suggestions, their retreat into the world of dreams were intensified and altered by the second generation. The dream gave way to "eternal" themes and motifs: God, the Sun, Eternity, and Fire.[18] The breach between the two groups widened into a schism, and the writers clashed in print. Brjusov felt that "Symbolism wanted to be and could be only art" and that "art [was] autonomous, having its own methods and tasks."[19] Vjačeslav Ivanov countered with the assertion that ". . . Symbolism did not want [to be] 'only art.'"[20] The first generation "clarists," in the person of Brjusov, endorsed clarity of thought, vocabulary, and imagery and fought against the mystics, who wanted poetry to serve as religion.[21] Brjusov accused Belyj, Ivanov, and their followers of creating art that receded ever further from life and said that they were sinking, on one hand, into archeology and, on the other, into mysticism.[22]

Belyj, perhaps the most important theoretician among the younger poets, echoed Blok in stressing the primacy of the symbol in poetry. He considered it many-faceted, representing variously an image of the visible, an allegory expressing the ideological sense of an image, or a call to the creation of life.[23] Belyj conjectured that the poet was a seer, a "spirit soaring over the chaos of sounds."[24]   The symbol always stood for *something* in Belyj's artistic theory, this *something* an undefined quality that pointed to a special reality in the realm of mysticism.[25] Konstantin Močul'skij has correctly noted that Belyj developed this philosophy not only in his theoretical writings, but in his poetry as well.[26]

The breach between the two Symbolist groups not only weakened the movement irrevocably, with the Acmeists and Futurists supplying the "coup de grace," but can also be seen as symptomatic of the rebellion for its own sake that characterized the modern movement. The last issue of the Symbolist journal *Vesy* appeared in December, 1909, and by 1910 Symbolism had ceased to function as a school.[27]   But the alternation of orientation and technique symptomatic of literary change ensured that the heirs of Symbolism might well be hostile to the later Symbolists, and Brjusov's discrediting of mystical Symbolism helped heighten this possibility.[28]   Brjusov's importance for the Acmeists was to be superceded only by the impact of Annenskij, cultural "anchor" for the school.

The   Acmeist and Futurist schools filled the vacuum left by the demise of the Symbolist movement, the simultaneous emergence of two such radically different groups indicative of the rapidity of change   by   1910.   Futurism   erupted   as   a   characteristically twentieth-century movement, a stylistic shock wave that hit Russia between 1910 and 1912, and Futurism was the implacable enemy of all preceding literary schools.[29]

The Russian Futurists, like the Symbolists, were divided into two   groups,   the   Ego-Futurists   of   St.   Petersburg   and   the Cubo-Futurists of Moscow.[30]   The Ego-Futurists were the less innovative of the two and were attracted to the neo-Romanticism of such late nineteenth-century poets as Konstantin Fofanov and Mirra Loxvickaja. Igor'-Severjanin [Igor' Vasil'evič Lotarev] , leader of the Ego-Futurists, displayed an affinity for foreign-sounding words and exotic objects in his later verse.[31]   The title of his 1911 collection, *Èlektričeskie stixi* (*Electric Verses*) exemplified the urban, contemporary leanings of this branch of Futurism.   Like others of his group, Igor'-Severjanin experimented with neologisms, rhyme, and the avoidance of logical links between words.[32]

Descended   from   the   Gileja   (Hylaea)   group   of   poets,   the Cubo-Futurists of Moscow divorced themselves from the urban orientation of the Ego-Futurists to embrace primitivist, rural subject matter.   The split between them and the Ego-Futurists is but one instance of the cultural schism between Western Petersburg and Russian Moscow.[33] The Cubo-Futurists, including such notables as Vladimir Majakovskij, Velemir [Viktor] Xlebnikov, the brothers David and Nikolaj Burljuk, Benedikt Livšic, and Aleksej Kručenyx, signed a manifesto in 1912. They broke all ties with preceding literature and spoke out for experimentation in poetic language.[34]

Like the early Symbolists, the Futurists initially looked to the West, specifically to the Italian school of the same name. The principal Italian theoretician, Filippe Marinetti, had published his manifesto in the February 20, 1909 issue of *Figaro*. The Italian Futurists proclaimed themselves citizens of the contemporary city, "new men" who espoused extreme change in the form of a dual cult of urbanism and military glory. Their Russian confrères eschewed militarism and channeled their rebelliousness into literature, asserting themselves as linguistic radicals who wanted to throw away existing culture, stressing sound over meaning in "transsense language."[35] While the Symbolists attempted to lose themselves in revolution, the Futurists instead identified themselves with its uncontrolled surge and embraced it on a conscious level. They harnessed themselves to revolutionary energy and sought to direct cataclysmic change, to control the enormous forces being unleashed. But they ultimately failed when these forces devoured them.[36]

Their repudiation of Puškin and their own contemporaries has been seen more as a means of drawing attention to their movement than as an expression of their aesthetic beliefs.[37] Because they viewed themselves as experimenters creating a completely new art, this is not really the case. The Cubo-Futurists, the more important by far of the two segments of the movement, were linked to brilliant experiments in the plastic arts, notably in Cubist and Rayonist painting and in Constructivism; both of the Burljuk brothers were painters, and Majakovskij painted before he wrote poetry. The avant-garde artists' emphasis on form and repudiation of all previous content, of all tradition, were connected, for it was not possible to create new forms while burdened with the legacy of the past, especially with a past strongly identified with Petersburg. They advocated constant change without the content of the past, change that combined experimentation with primitivism. Their only possible allegiance would be to a philosophy that was itself the embodiment of that change, the Revolution.

It was the Acmeists alone who, reacting against both the Symbolists and Futurists, sought a thread of continuity with tradition, knowing instinctively that total change completely cut off from the past, the cultural center, would mean the annihilation of that culture. And hence they maintained their ties as a coping mechanism, a means of survival, with their doctrine a declaration of ideals in a period when civilization seemed to be surrendering to its antithesis.[38] If the Symbolists and Futurists were centrifugal forces, then the Acmeists were centripedal, hence, their apparent conservatism.

The Acmeists regarded themselves as heirs of the older Symbolists and repudiated the mysticism and lack of clarity peculiar to the younger ones. The disaffected Symbolist poet Mixail Kuzmin prepared the ground for the first Acmeist theoretical works with his essay "O prekrasnoj jasnosti" ("On Beautiful Clarity"), published in 1910.[39] Kuzmin coupled his call for a return to logical, clear expression with the suggestion that the perfection of literary style was a goal in itself.[40] The Acmeists developed these ideas more extensively in their first theoretical writings, Nikolaj Gumilev's essay "Zavety simvolizma i akmeizm" ("The Precepts of Symbolism, and Acmeism") and Sergej Gorodeckij's "Nekotorye tečenija v sovremennoj russkoj poèzii" ("Some Currents in Contemporary Russian Poetry"). With its "return" to aesthetic values predating later Symbolism, Acmeism would seem to represent a somewhat conservative movement in poetic expression, a sort of throwback to the poetic practice dominant in Russian letters before the advent of realism. But the link they sought to maintain had never been completely severed; it had remained viable in the poetic practice and theoretical writings, indeed in the very personality, of their mentor, Innokentij Fedorovič Annenskij. He was the sole writer of the period who functioned as a bridge between the aesthetic standards and values of Puškin's time and the experimentation that was the hallmark of modernism.

Born in the mid-1850s, Annenskij was older than the other modernist poets.[41] He died of a heart attack on November 30, 1909.[42] Annenskij made his poetic debut late in life, in the early 1900s; *Tixie pesni* (*Quiet Songs*), the only collection of verse to appear in his lifetime, was published in 1904. It included an appendix of translated poems from the "Parnascy i prokljatye" ("Parnassians and Accursed Ones," the Parnassians and French

Symbolists) and was signed with the pseudonym "Nik. T-o," an anagram for "nikto," "nobody."[43]   His second, posthumous collection, *Kiparisovyj larec* (*The Cypress Chest*), appeared in 1910.[44]

In his refusal to align himself with a particular school, namely Symbolism, Annenskij was unique among modernist Russian poets.   Certain Symbolist stylistic elements, such as the use of suggestion and the incorporation of the themes of dream and death, are evident in his work.   But his tastes were catholic; he drew on those aspects of earlier and contemporary literature that seemed most appropriate.   Because he earned his living as a teacher of classical languages and literatures, he could tap this background as well.[45]

While linked provisionally with Symbolism by his use of suggestion and some of his poetic motifs, Annenskij nevertheless should be considered divorced from the movement.   He did not consciously sever himself from nineteenth-century verse and displayed certain affinities with earlier poets. He was connected with Puškin through their joint association with Tsarskoe Selo.[46] Annenskij also resembled his predecessor in the importance he attached to art, his assertion that the poet hold himself aloof from philistinism, and in his conciseness and use of prosaisms.[47] Annenskij, like Puškin, refused to sever himself from either Russian or Western culture and drew on both.   Annenskij exhibited similarities to Evgenij Baratynskij, focusing pessimistically on autumn, sadness, and death.[48]   Like Afanasij Fet, he used nature principally as a backdrop for the projection of a mood or general mental state,[49] and the works of both poets are marked by concreteness of perception, most often through nature.[50]   Fedor Tjutčev, whose metaphysical verse was important for the Symbolists, had a twofold impact on Annenskij.   Not only were the palpable images of each poet intended as a foil for philosophical complexity, but Annenskij was also heir to Tjutčev's philosophical lyricism.   Undoubtedly both were affected by the poetry of Baratynskij.[51]

Because he never broke with the civic poets thematically but instead exhibited a perceptible resemblance to them, Annenskij was separate even from the first generation of Symbolists.[52] Like the civic poets, he displayed an awareness of social injustice in a number of his lyrics, and in three poems, "V doroge" ("On the Road"), "Kartinka" ("The Little Picture"), and "Opjat' v doroge"

("On the Road Again"), he expressed sympathy for the lot of the peasants and guilt over his own relative cultural and material prosperity.[53]   In "Ijul'" ("July"), Annenskij commented bitterly on the dehumanization of men working on a road.[54]

Annenskij's concern for social injustice extended to an interest in political problems, a typical reaction in the Russia of his time. In the lyric "Peterburg" ("Petersburg"), first published in the journal *Apollon* (*Apollo*) in 1910, he evoked the sensation of unreality with which the city had been associated in Puškin's poem "Mednyj vsadnik" ("The Bronze Horseman"), Nikolaj Gogol's stories "Nos" ("The Nose") and "Šinel'" ("The Overcoat"), the works of Dostoevskij, and Belyj's novel *Peterburg* (*Petersburg*). Annenskij returned to Puškin's image of St. Petersburg (and, by extension, the modern Russian state) as a mirage existing as a result of an imperial command.[55]   "Nervy (Plastinka dlja grammofona)" ("Nerves [A Record for the Grammophone]") contains a stream-of-consciousness description of parents' realization that their son has been arrested. The note of despair Annenskij sounds in this lyric is similar to the tone of pessimism and helplessness in his poems on the social limitations of the peasants.[56]

In "Starye èstonki" ("Old Estonian Women"), Annenskij directly equated political tyranny with social inequality. The poem was inspired by events of October, 1905 in Estonia, where several participants in a workers' demonstration were killed and eighty-nine others severely wounded,[57] and it contains Annenskij's most open criticism of the regime of Nikolaj II.[58]

His interest in social and political questions might very well have resulted from the influence of his older brother, Nikolaj Fedorovič Annenskij, who reared the poet following the deaths of their parents. A popular journalist, Nikolaj Fedorovič was a public figure, a man of democratic views.[59]   Annenskij's pedagogical work, as evinced by the large number of articles and book reviews in which he dealt with this subject, may also have predisposed him to a certain degree of social awareness.[60]   As a man of wide interests ranging from classical Greek literature and linguistics to contemporary Russian literature, it would not have been unreasonable for him to have been aware of current social and political questions.   In his solicitude for sufferers from social injustice, he exhibited an orientation toward the real, physical world, a view that would also find an outlet in his verse and in the Acmeists' doctrinal essays.[61]

Annenskij's conscious identification with his immediate predecessors bespeaks two things. He obviously viewed himself as a link in a chain of cultural achievement as expressed in literature, a link connecting him with Russian literature as well as that of the West. Of equal significance is the fact that he never cut himself off from the physical world in which he lived, never took refuge either in a narcissistic view of himself as the poet apart from reality (as did the early Symbolists) or in a mystical attempt to transcend (which tendency defines the later ones). These two factors were both to have enormous significance for the Acmeists, who viewed themselves as continuators of a civilization that existed in a real world.

According to L. Ja. Ginzburg, there is a complex analogy between Annenskij's verse and contemporary psychological and realistic prose; the connection between Annenskij and Čexov is especially marked in the interplay of feelings and conversational cues and nuances.[62] (This similarity is indicative of the fact, mentioned above, that prose was forced to take on a lyrical role that had been abdicated by civic poetry.) Annenskij's affinity with Čexov may also be seen in the tone of self-irony that forms an undercurrent in many lyrics.[63] These links underscore metaphysical differences between Annenskij and the early Symbolists, for whom poetic creation was by definition separate and different from the realistic, "prosaic" tendencies of the civic poets.

Annenskij's intimate acquaintance with nineteenth-century Russian poetry and contemporary Russian literature did not preclude an awareness of Western European literatures. Georgij Adamovič has asserted that Annenskij was in fact the only truly European figure of Russian modernism.[64] In an obituary notice on the poet, B. Varneke remarked on Annenskij's predilection for French culture, noting that the deceased ". . . often talked about how he would have turned out if fate had allowed him to live for a year in Paris—there he sensed native soil. His favorite journal was the *Mercure de France* and, however he loved Puškin, the French were closer to his soul."[65]

The Parnassians, together with the Symbolist Paul Verlaine, had a significant impact on Annenskij, "a brilliant connoisseur . . . of the poetry of the French 'Parnasse' . . . ."[66] He shared with them a cult of poetic form and a love of the word as such.[67] Considering his views on the intrinsic value of art (to be examined later), it is scarcely surprising that Annenskij was drawn to the Parnassians. It was the poet Théophile Gautier, one of the young Romantics of 1830, who initiated the theory of art for art's sake in 1835 in the preface to his novel *Mademoiselle de Maupin*, a theory he restated in his principal volume of poems *Émaux et Camées* in 1852.[68]   The Parnassians stressed impersonality in rather static verse that was painstakingly composed and expressed a renewed interest in the classical world, an interest that would later inform the work of both Annenskij and Mandel'štam.

Annenskij was drawn to the French Symbolists as well, resembling them in his view that Symbolism (and art in general) was an aesthetic complex.[69]   Like the French *poètes maudits* (Symbolists), he considered man a "plaything of nature," an "episode in the chain of godless world creation." Sergej Makovskij noted that Annenskij, not without justification, felt himself a follower of Mallarmé, Rimbaud, and Verlaine who regarded man as being at the mercy of all-powerful time.[70]

Like Brjusov, Annenskij derived his stylistic method and many of his devices from the French Symbolists, stating in his essay "O sovremennom lirizme" ("On Contemporary Lyricism") that he did not want a single, universal meaning for poetry.[71]   He partially followed the French in making suggestion the basis of his verse, subscribing to an extent to Mallarmé's dictum that to name was to destroy while to suggest was to create.[72]

His stylistic link with French Symbolism extended beyond the mere employment of suggestion in verse, for like the French he concentrated a lyrical theme in one symbolically treated subject or in a complex of interconnected ones.[73]   Although he used the symbol and suggestion, Annenskij's compression of a lyrical theme within one subject or related subjects lent greater clarity and hence impact to what might otherwise have produced a rather diffuse impression.   Annenskij borrowed other stylistic devices from the French, and Makovskij has asserted that "Annenskij alone, of all the Russian poets, understood the fine points of French syllabo-tonic [verse] structure faultlessly."[74]

Annenskij exhibited a lively interest in individual French Symbolists, being drawn especially to Charles Baudelaire, a intimacy reflected in his poetry.[75]   Like Baudelaire, Annenskij used the metaphor extensively, employing it in personification and concretization.[76]   He was a follower of Baudelaire in matters of lexicon as well, combining "high," "poetic" speech with scholarly or scientific terminology and "everyday" words.[77]

Stéphane Mallarmé also had a considerable influence on Annenskij who had, more than anyone else in Russia, familiarized himself with the French poet.[78]   A twilight tone permeated the verse of both writers, who combined moods of inquietude and sadness with an awareness of the transcience of existence and the finality of death.[79]   Like Mallarmé, Annenskij consciously rendered the intellectual content of a poem unclear by constructing it like a rebus, forcing the reader to penetrate the images to grasp the internal structure and meaning.[80]

The impact of Paul Verlaine on Annenskij was greater than that of any other French poet, however.[81]   Verlaine advocated a musicality of verse in which poetry would be turned into a "melodic rain of symbols,"[82] and Annenskij is supposed to have subscribed to Verlaine's concept that music occupied the primary place in poetry; he partially followed this dictum in his verse by attempting to express an "emotional attitude" in much the same way that a composer does in a musical work.[83]   Unfortunately Annenskij, along with several of the early Symbolists, arrived at the same distortion of Verlaine's theory as did the French aesthetician Téodor de Wyzewa.   Wyzewa alleged that the idea of musicality in poetry referred only to the sounds of words and did not have to be merged with other elements in speech, thus going counter to Verlaine's basic idea.   Both French and Russian critics established an artificial dichotomy in which poetry was an intellectual utterance and music an emotional one.   Annenskij asserted that the "musical potentiality of the word is necessary. . . in order to provoke a creative mood in the readers. . . ."[84] Annenskij's conception is interesting in view of his emphasis on visual images rather than sound, a subject to be treated more extensively in subsequent chapters.

Annenskij's orientation toward Western Europe was further evidenced by his mastery of Greek and Latin and of classical literature.   His delight in his Italian travels reflects a mind that felt at ease in the West.[85]   His attitude was unusual among cultivated Russians of his time, for even the early Symbolists had looked to their French counterparts solely because the French were, at that time, the only poets on whom they could model themselves.   The later Symbolists turned inward, back to Orthodox roots (through Vladimir Solov'ev) and Russian culture (as seen in the work of Blok and Belyj).

This alternation of Russian/Western, characterizing Russian literature from the time of Peter the Great and increasing in intensity during the nineteenth century, continued during the modernist period, not only in Symbolism, but among the Acmeists as well. The Acmeists, rebelling against the Symbolists, again looked outward, directing their attention variously to exotic locales in the case of Gumilev, to the classical Mediterranean world in the case of Mandel'štam. The Acmeists found a mentor in Annenskij, the one Russian poet with the range sophisticated enough for him to have drawn on both Russian and Western models.

Annenskij's relationship with the Russian Symbolists and his position vis-à-vis Symbolism are of necessity ambiguous, Brjusov himself having charged Annenskij with not resembling other poets.[86] L. Ja. Ginzburg stated that there was an absence of any kind of organizational tie or even any close relationship between Annenskij and the representatives of the "new poetry."[87] Because he maintained a separate identity in an environment in which all poets belonged to one or another school while he held himself aloof, Annenskij could only be regarded as "different" and, probably, suspect. His separateness eerily foreshadows the literary and related political isolation of two of the principal Acmeists, Axmatova and Mandel'štam, who held themselves apart from the political turmoil that wracked literature in Stalin's time, yet refused to emigrate. Annenskij's conception of the artist as a non-aligned individual for whom art itself was central, a legacy of Puškin, was one of the most important gifts he passed on to the Acmeists. The impact of this self-image, developed in his poetry and essays, was to be central to the formation of the Acmeist doctrine.

CHAPTER TWO

THEMES IN ANNENSKIJ'S POETRY

A gifted but not prolific writer, Annenskij left a number of important critical articles, some book reviews, several original tragedies, and approximately five hundred lyrics. Because the themes in Annenskij's verse, illustrative of his world view and aesthetic values, clearly demonstrate his link with Acmeism, a discussion of them will constitute the nucleus of the present chapter.

Annenskij's poems can be categorized according to six major themes: death, life, dream, time, nature, and artistic creation, especially poetry. The lyrics best illustrating these themes will be analyzed in detail. The themes of death, life, dream, and nature are actually subordinate to that of time, which binds all of them together. It is in this very emphasis upon temporality that Annenskij is linked with the Acmeists and their acceptance of reality. Annenskij's exemption of artistic creation from the strictures of time is paralleled by the significance that art held for the Acmeists.

Death played an important role in the poems of the early Symbolists, particularly those of Konstantin Bal'mont and Sologub, for it was regarded as an alternative to a life without hope and was considered a means of escape.[1] Death was significant in Annenskij's work also. It was in his lyrics on this theme that he came closest to Symbolism. An analysis of "Siren' na kamne" ("Lilac on the Stone"), reproduced here in part, will serve as an example.

"Klubjatsja tuči sizocvetno
Moj put' dalek, moj put' unyl.
A dal' tak mutno-bezotvetna
Iz kraja serogo mogil.
Vot kem-to vrezan krest zamšennyj
V plite nadgrobnoj i, kak ten',

Skvoz' kamen', Lazar' voskrešennyj,
Probilas' čaxlaja siren'.

Listy požëlkli, obgoreli. . .
To gnët li neba, kamnja l' gnët, –
No govorjat, čto i v aprele
Siren' mogily ne cvetet.

. . . .

Už večer blizko. I puti
Peredo mnoj ešče tak mnogo,
No prosto sily net sojti
S zavorožennogo poroga."[2]

. . . .

"Dove-gray storm clouds are swirling.
My way is far, my way is sad.
And the distance is so dully-meek
From the gray edge of the graves.

There a moss-covered cross has been incised by someone
In the gravestone and, like a shadow,
Along the stone, Lazarus resurrected,
A stunted lilac has broken through.

The leaves have turned yellow, have been scorched. . .
Now [there is] the weight of heaven, now the weight of the
stone –
But it is said that, even in April
The lilac of a grave does not bloom.

. . . .

Already evening is near. And the ways
Before me are still so many,
But there is simply no strength to depart
From the charmed threshold."

. . . .

This lyric is curiously anticipatory of Robert Frost's "Stopping
by Woods on a Snowy Evening."   "Put'" ("Way," "Path") is a
common literary equivalent for life, while the obscurity of distance
suggests the unknown, the future and, by extension, death.   The
distance ends in the gray region of graves, with death posited as
an inevitable end to the long road of life and grayness a visual
symbol for colorless, lifeless death.   The gravestone itself with the

incised cross is linked with the lilac bush, which in turn is equated with Lazarus, a symbol for the state between life and death, more specifically, for the victory of life over death.

Lilac is further anthropomorphized in the next stanza, when it is associated with both the sky and the gravestone in much the way that man is in limbo between life and death. In spite of the infinity (sky) of the intellect and imagination, man is always forced to contemplate death (the gravestone). Knowledge of death poisons life: the leaves of the lilac have already become yellow, and the poet states that lilac growing over a tomb does not bloom even in April. Similarly, man must wither before his time, poisoned by the awareness that death is a constant companion on his journey through life—one that can conquer at any time. The verb "govorjat" ("they say") emphasizes that the affliction of impending death is universal. In addition to symbolizing the transcience of human life, lilac represents beauty and the life of the spirit, offering therefore the greatest possible contrast to death (the stone).

The approach of evening and multitude of available paths underscore the poet's awareness that one's choices in life are narrowed considerably by the realization of approaching death. This knowledge takes away the desire even to attempt to fulfill possibilities (to step off the threshold, as suggested in the fourth stanza cited). These lines again stress that the awareness of death thwarts the infinite possibilities of the intellect. Finally, Annenskij's realization that death is a physical, inescapable end is related to the Acmeists' acceptance of the limitations of the physical world, with the survival of his curiously stunted lilac a symbol of the strength of beauty (identified with art).

Life is one of Annenskij's important themes, Setchkarev having asserted that, along with "anxiety for the beautiful," it is his principal one.[3] The lyrics on life are less numerous than those on death, but they nevertheless include some vital examples. Poems about "toska" ("Depression," "melancholy," "yearning") dominate this category; "Toska" is illustrative of these.

"Po bledno-rozovym ovalam,
Tumanom utra oblity,
Svilis' buketom nebyvalym
Stal'nogo kólera cvety.

I mux kočujuščix soblazny,
Otravu v gljance zataja,

Pestrjat, nazojlivy i prazdny,
Nagie grani bytija.

No, lixoradkoju tomimyj,
Kogda nedeljami ležiš',
V odnoobraz'i ix taimyj
Pojmeš' ty sladostnyj gašiš.

Pojmeš, na gljance centrifolij
Sčitaja berežno mazki. . .
I stroja romby ponevole
Meždu ètapami Toski."[4]

"Along the pale-rose ovals,
Glazed by the mist of morning,
Flowers of a steely hue
Were coiled in a fantastic bouquet.

And the temptations of roaming flies,
Harboring poison in [their] lustre,
Show rainbow-colored, troublesome, and idle,
The naked boundaries of existence.

But, wearied by fever,
When you are lying for weeks,
Will you comprehend sweet hashish
In their hidden monotony.

Will you comprehend, in the lustre of the centrefoils
Considering cautiously the dabs [of the brush]. . .
And building rhombuses willy-nilly
Among the halting-places of melancholy."

The persona in "Toska" is an invalid, an observer in a physically limited world, his feverish exhaustion implying existence in an unnatural realm suspended between life and death and resembling the lilac of "Siren' na kamne." The wallpaper in his room is covered with a pattern of ovals around which bouquets of flowers are entwined. Annenskij's use of the word "nebyvalyj" ("fantastic," "imaginary"), his employment of the word "kóler" (a painter's term suggesting artifice, indicative of Annenskij's visual orientation), with the steel-colored flowers stresses the artificiality of the invalid's world. The invalid here is everyman, prey to the banal power of life.[5]

The "Temptations of roaming flies" are the wallpaper flowers of the preceding stanza. The association of bees and butterflies with living flowers is juxtaposed to the swarming flies around the rigid pattern of the wallpaper flowers, thereby emphasizing both the unnaturalness of the "nature" surrounding the persona and the poison that the flies harbor. In the last line of the second stanza, the poet speaks of the "naked boundaries of existence," once again equating the rigid limitations of life with the wallpaper pattern.

Annenskij's frequent use of participles in "Toska" cuts off both persona and reader from the normal world of action, imprisoning them in a static realm. In the first stanza, where the flowers have been glazed by the mist of morning (". . .cvety . . .tumanom utra oblity"), the "action" of the mist, having been deprived of its force, now merely describes the flowers. As a result of Annenskij's use of this participle, the objects of the poem, normally fixtures of reality, have been removed grammatically from that sphere of existence and have become part of an artificial world. Annenskij has grammatically stressed the fact that "toska" represents in capsule form the artificiality of life, symbolizing life's negation. His pessimism is therefore linked with his emphasis on death and his awareness of the limitations of life. The participle, in addition, makes an image more tangible, closer to the visual world of the Acmeists.

Because dreams symbolize escape from reality, they were a common theme in the poetry of the Russian Symbolists.[6] Dream occupies a special place in Annenskij's poetry also, representing a world divorced from the limitations of time, an alternative existence for the poet.[7] Annenskij's dream poems can be divided into three categories: loss of orientation, oblivion, and nightmare. They will be dealt with in this order, with "Dvojnik" ("The Double") considered first.

"Ne ja, i ne on, i ne ty,
No to že, čto ja, i ne to že:
Tak byli my gde-to poxoži,
Čto naši smešalis' čerty.

V somnen'i kipit ešče spor,
No, slity nezrimoj četoju,
Odnoj my živem i mečtoju,
Mečtoju razluki s tex por.

Gorjačešnyj son volnoval
Obmanom vtoryx očertanij,

No čem ja gljadel neustannej,
Tem jarče sebja ž uznaval.

Liš' pologa noči nemoj
Poroj otrazit kolyxan'e
Moe i drugoe dyxan'e,
Boj serdca i moj i ne moj. . .

I v mutnom kružen'i godin
Vsë čašče vopros menja mučit:
Kogda nakonec nas razlučat,
Kakim že ja budu odin?"[8]

"Not I, and not he, and not thou,
But the same as I, and not the same;
Thus were we somewhere similar,
So that our features were merged.

An argument still simmers in the doubt,
But, fused as an invisible pair,
We live by a single dream,
By the dream of separation from those times.

The most ardent dream was agitated
By a deception of second outlines,
But the more I peered, tireless,
The more vividly I recognized myself.

At times the swing of the [bed] curtains
Of dumb night
Only reflects my breathing and that of another
The beating of a heart that is both mine and not mine. . .

And in the turbid whirling of time
The question torments me ever more often:
When at last they will separate us,
What will I be alone?"

Annenskij has blurred here the primary differentiation of identity, that between the persona and the external world, the "I" and the "non-I." In the first line, the first, second, and third persons have been deliberately confused, thereby destroying the normal distinctions of conversation and narration, indeed, of existence. Nothing is certain, not even the distinct separateness of the individual consciousness. The blurring of the line between the self and others is but an individual version of the concurrent and frightening changes in society. (The loneliness of the persona is

found also in Čexov's characters, thus underscoring the link
between the two writers.)   Having altered the reader's perception
of the actual world, Annenskij has placed the rest of the poem
outside   reality by erasing the conceptions of definite time and
space in addition to that of identity.   All existence, shorn of
limiting definition, has been transformed into a dream.
    Oblivion represents separation from reality, the cessation of
time.   The lyric "Kogda b ne smert', a zabyt'e" ("If there were
not death, but oblivion") exemplifies such a state.

"Kogda b ne smert', a zabyt'e,
Čtob ni dviženija, ni zvuka. . .
Ved' esli vslušat'sja v nee,
Vsja žizn' moja - ne žizn', a muka.

Il' ja ne s vami taju, dni?
Ne vjanu s list'jami na klenax?
Il' ne moi umrut ogni
V slezax kristallov rastoplennyx?

Il' ja ne ves' v bezljud'e skal
I černom niščenstve berezy?
Ne ves' v tom belom puxe rozy,
Čto xolod utra okoval?

V doždinkax ètix, čto navisli,
Čtob žemčugami nispadat'? . .
A mne, skažite, v mukax mysli
Najdetsja l' serdce sostradat'?"[9]

If there were not death, but oblivion,
So that there were neither movement, nor noise. . .
If one really would listen attentively to it,
My entire life - is not life, but torment.

Or do I not wane with you, days?
Do I not fade with the leaves on the maples?
Or do my fires not die
In the tears of melting crystals?

Or am I not all in the desolateness of rocks
And in the black beggary of the birch?
Not all in that white down of the rose,
That the cold of morning fettered?

In these drops of rain, that have hung over,
In order to fall as pearls?

But for me, tell me, in the torments of thought
Will a heart be found to be compassionate?"

Annenskij has posited a dichotomy here between thought,
culminating in consciousness of personal annihilation, or death, and
oblivion. Oblivion is loss of awareness, specifically of the awareness
of time and its ultimate conclusion. It is the ability to blend
oneself with nature, to fade with the autumn leaves, wane with the
days, melt with melting crystals. As with his other nature poems,
his emphasis here is on dying nature, surely a metaphysical
statement, an expression of his general pessimism. Annenskij's
pessimism has two roots: he feels anguish for the destruction of
beauty, symbolized here by melting crystals, and he suffers at his
separation from the natural world, from which he is severed by his
"torment of thought." His pain is paradoxical, since the very
thought enabling him to be cognizant of and to appreciate beauty
simultaneously causes the rift concomitant with his subservience to
time. The melting crystals stand for the visual, ultimately planar
structures that Annenskij identified with art. They will reappear
in other lyrics, juxtaposed to the indefiniteness of Symbolist poetry.
    An element of terror distinguishes nightmare from both the
loss of orientation and oblivion. Threatening the sufferer with
death, the nightmare is vividly real. "Utro" ("Morning") is a
striking example of such a state.

"Èta noč' beskonečna byla,
Ja ne smel, ja bojalsja usnut':
Dva mučitel'no-černyx kryla
Tjaželo mne ložilis' na grud'.

Na prizyvy ž tex kryl'ev v otvet
Trepetal, zamiraja, ptenec,
I ne znal ja, pridet li rassvet
Ili èto už polnyj konec. . .

O, smelee. . .Košmar pozadi,
Ego strašnoe carstvo prošlo;
Vešix ptic na grudi i v grudi
Otšumelo do zavtra krylo. . .

Oblaka ešče plačut, gudja,
No svetleet i nexotja ten',
I banal'nyj, za set'ju doždja,

Ulybnut'sja poproboval Den'."[10]

"This night was endless,
I did not dare, I was afraid to go to sleep:
Two agonizingly-black wings
Lay down heavily on my chest.

The nestling quivered, growing still
In answer to the appeal of those wings,
And I did not know whether dawn would come
Or if this was already the absolute end. . .

Oh, bolder. . .The Nightmare is behind,
Its terrible kingdom has passed;
The wing of the prophetic birds on and in my chest
Has stopped making noise until the morrow. . .

The clouds are still weeping, droning,
But the shadow reluctantly brightens up,
And banal Day, behind a net of rain,
Made an attempt to smile."

By blurring the distinction between dream and reality, Annenskij has reproduced the terror of the nightmare, for the reader cannot tell if the persona is really having a bad dream, or if he is instead having a heart attack. Annenskij's use of the color black, the fact that the night was "endless," and the sensation that "prophetic birds" were making noise on top and inside of his chest could denote either physical sufferings or the nightmare itself.[11] The "Day" at the end of the poem, not merely a unit of time, is a symbol for the force of light against the power of darkness, good against evil, life against death. Its feebleness is a reflection of Annenskij's pessimism, a common feature in the poetry of his time.

While Annenskij's employment of the dream to represent a world at least temporarily outside the ravages of time is common to Symbolism as well, he differs from his contemporaries in allowing the intrusion of reality to negate the escape value of the dream. The poet is thus forced to follow another route in his struggle with time, and that route, poetry, will be discussed below.

As the background against which thought and emotion can be projected and as an external mirror of human existence, nature constitutes a significant theme in Annenskij's verse. The winter poem "Sneg" ("Snow") will be considered here.

"Poljubil by ja zimu,
Da obuza tjažka. . .
Ot nee daže dymu
Ne ujti v oblaka.

Èta rezannost' linij,
Ètot gruznyj polet,
Ètot niščenski sinij
I zaplakannyj led!

No ljublju oslabelyj
Ot zaoblačnyx neg –
To sverkajušče belyj
To sirenevyj sneg. . .

I osobenno talyj,
Kogda, vysi otkryv,
On ložitsja ustalyj
Na skol'zjaščij obryv,

Točno stado v tumane
Neporočnye sny –
Na tomitel'noj grani
Vsesožžen'ja vesny."[12]

"I would love winter,
But the burden is heavy. . .
Not even smoke can escape from it
Into the clouds.

This incising of lines,
This cumbersome flight,
This beggarly dark–blue
And tear–stained ice!

But I love the snow weakened
From blisses beyond the clouds –
The snow now sparkling white
Now sparkling lilac. . .

And especially melting [snow],
When, having opened the heights,
It lies down tired
On the sliding precipice;

The chaste dreams
Are like flocks in the mist –
On the oppressive brink
Of the holocaust of spring."

"Sneg" is graced by sharpness of lines, by the specificity resulting from the repeated use of the definite demonstrative adjective "èto" ("this"), and by a marked contrast in the lines and colors that denote a distinction between one shape and another. Annenskij's use of oxymoron ("heavy clouds," "weeping ice") make his images even sharper. In his emphasis on the clarity of lines and colors, Annenskij demonstrates the very aesthetic principles later set forth by the Acmeists, who themselves stressed color, line, and form. It should be noted that "Sneg" was first published in *Apollon* late in Annenskij's career, after he had already brought out critical essays in what was to become the Acmeist journal.[13] The region above the clouds, emblematic of the imagined realm beyond the reach of the senses, is hinted at but not attained.

Annenskij's critical essays were not the only medium for his aesthetic views, which figured also in his metapoetry. He anticipated the Acmeists in considering the poet a creator of clear, linear art, in contrast to the amorphousness of the later Symbolists. His divergence from Symbolism is especially marked in "Poètu" ("To the Poet").

"V razdel'noj četkosti lučej
I čadnoj slitnosti videnij
Vsegda nad nami – vlast' veščej
S ee triadoj izmerenij.

. . . .

Ta vlast' majak, zovet ona,
V nej sočetalis' Bog i tlennost',
I pered neju tak bledna
Veščej v iskusstve prikrovennost'.

. . . .

Krasa otkrytogo lica
Vlekla Orfeja pieridy.
Užel' dostojny vy pevca,
Pokrovy kukol'noj Izidy?

Ljubi razdel'nost' i luči
V roždennom imi aromate.
Ty čaši jarkie toči
Dlja celokupnyx vosprijatij."[14]

"In the separate clearness of rays
And in the smoky fusing of visions
The power of things, with its triad of measurements,
Is always over us.

. . . .

That power is a beacon, she calls,
God and perishability have been combined in it,
And the essence of things in art
So pale, is before it.

. . . .

The beauty of the open [revealed] face
Attracted Orpheus of the Pierides.
Are you, shrouds of the doll-like Isis,
Really worthy of the singer?

Love separateness [distinctness] and rays
In the fragrance generated by them.
Grind thou brilliant chalices
For integral perceptions."

     Intended as a lesson on how to write verse, this lyric is part of a Russian tradition of metapoetry going back to Puškin. "Poètu" can be considered a set of instructions to the Acmeists themselves, with the "power of things" telling the apprentice poet how to write. Throughout, Annenskij focuses on the importance of clarity and concreteness, juxtaposing them to abstraction and indefiniteness, and expressing aesthetic views that the Acmeists would later espouse.

     In the first stanza, the "power of things" measures with her triad in the "separate clearness of rays" and in the "smoky fusing of visions." Annenskij's assertion that poetry is a "science" governed by certain laws, exact within limits, is suggested by the presence of the measuring triad of dimensions. The female figure with the triad stands for the muse, who in turn symbolizes the art of classical Greece with its orientation toward clarity and the beauty of the visual image; Annenskij thereby further demonstrates his link with classical cultures. The exactness of art is further exemplified in the first line by the "separate clearness of rays," in which the power of things dwells. The words "nad nami" ("over us") in the third line allude to the poet in the title and the persona, and the implication of the stanza as a whole is that poets (the "we" of the third line) are responsible for creating clear verse. The power of things suggests, therefore, that the poets are craftsmen.[15]

The reference to Orpheus and his predilection for the beauty of the open face echoes the allusion to the muse in the first stanza. Like the muse, Orpheus symbolizes the art of classical Greece, an art in which the achievement of beautiful form is posited as the highest goal.[16] The beauty of the open face might refer to the muse, or it could also stand for the brilliant achievement of Greek sculpture, the highest accomplishment in the plastic arts in Greece and a symbol of the solid, physical world.[17]

The Egyptian goddess Isis was a fantastic spirit only remotely similar to human beings; her veil ("shrouds") symbolizes her mysterious essence and suggests a lack of clarity and definitive form as well. The enigmatic appearance of the Egyptian deities, combined with their dimly understood actions (in contrast to those of the Greek gods), is also symbolized by Isis' veil, which screens her off from human perception and speculation. Since mystery and distortion are divorced from clarity and can never by aesthetically pleasing in the way that natural beauty can, Annenskij deprives Isis of life by calling her a doll.

But Isis has a more immediate significance. She might very well stand for the figure of Eternal Wisdom that first appeared in Solov'ev's philosophy and was later developed in the beautiful and then damned lady of Aleksandr Blok. Annenskij's condemnation of her in the form of Isis is indicative of his attitude toward the poetry of the later Symbolists, who felt that beauty must be disguised and disfigured to be significant, i.e., transcend the everyday world.

In the last stanza, which parallels the first, Annenskij once more addresses the apprentice poet of the title and stanza one. He exhorts him to love separateness and rays [of light], symbols of visual clarity and structural beauty.[18] In the last two lines, the poet "grinds brilliant chalices for integral perceptions," implying that he is a craftsman who creates beautiful form to contain his perceptions. Active rather than passive, the poet is not merely an intermediary between the earth and a higher realm; he is not a seer or transmitter, but a creator.[19]

At first glance, Annenskij seems ambiguous about the capacity of an individual work of art to survive the death of the artist. In some lyrics, he seems to be suggesting that art becomes, in a sense, eternal, while creating the impression in others that the work of art endures only while being created. This apparent contradiction can be cleared up readily by examining two poems, "Bronzovyj poèt" ("The Bronze Poet") and "Posle koncerta" ("After the Concert"). In the former, he stresses the eternality of art.

"Na sinem kupole belejut oblaka,
I četko vvys' ušli kudrjavye veršiny,
No pyl' už svetitsja, a teni stali dlinny,
I k serdcu prizraki plyvut izdaleka.

Ne znaju, povest' li byla tak korotka,
Il' ja ne dočital poslednej poloviny? . .
Na blednom kupole pogasli oblaka,
I noč' uže idet skvoz' černye veršiny. . .

I stali - i skam'ja i čelovek na nej
V nedvižnom sumrake tjažele i strašnej.
Ne ševelis' - sejčas gvozdiki zasverkajut,

Vozdušnye kusty sol'jutsja i rastajut,
I bronzovyj poèt, strjaxnuv dremoty gnet,
S podstavki na travu rosistuju sprygnët."[20]

"The clouds gleam white on the dark-blue dome
And the leafy tree-tops have receded clearly into the heights,
But dust is already glowing, and the shadows have grown long,
And phantoms are gliding toward the heart from afar.
I do not know, if the tale was so brief,
Or if I did not finish reading the second half? . . .
The clouds have gone out on the dome,
And night is already coming through the black tree-tops.
And both the bench and the person on it
Became heavier and more terrible in the motionless twilight.
Do not stir - the carnations will begin to sparkle shortly,
The aerial bushes will flow together and fade,
And the bronze poet, having shaken off the weight of his
drowsiness,
Will jump from his pedestal onto the dewy grass."

The dark-blue cupola of the sky with white clouds drifting across it is equated with the cupolas of Russian Orthodox churches, which are painted blue with golden stars. With this image, Annenskij establishes a link between poetry and architecture, a connection that would be of cardinal importance in Mandel'štam's essay "Utro akmeizma" ("The Morning of Acmeism"), and in his poetry as well.[21]

Evening has given way to night by the second stanza, with the narrator's sense of time distorted or absent. (In the first two lines, he confesses that he does not know if he has seen a segment of an event or has been witness to an entire event of short duration.) He suddenly realizes that the clouds on the pale cupola have gone out ("pogasli"). Like "belet'" ("to appear white"), the verb "pogasnut'" ("to go out") emphasizes the ephemeral brightness of the clouds and their similarity to stars. Once again the sky is called a cupola (dome) with the implied comparison to a church. Both "pogasli" ("went out," "have gone out") and "uže" ("already") in the last line suggest a sudden change noticed only after it has occurred. Like the abrupt transition from evening to night, these words suspend the normal measurement of time. The sense of timelessness evoked by the verbs, the symbolic eternality of the Orthodox Church, and the sky now function as a backdrop for the event that will transpire in the third stanza.

A man and bench suddenly appear in stanza three, the abruptness with which they have become visible emphasized by the suspended time of the second stanza and by the verb "stali" ("became") at the beginning of the third. The man, actually a statue of Aleksandr Puškin by R. Bach, is located in the park in Tsarskoe Selo.[22] Tsarskoe Selo was associated with Puškin and came to be a symbol for the classical restraint characterizing his verse and later the poetry of Annenskij and Axmatova. It is a "realm of poetry" spanning the nineteenth and twentieth centuries, symbolizing the union of art and timelessness just as the dome of the sky does.

In stanza four, the statue of Puškin has shaken off its weight and jumped from its pedestal onto the grass. Annenskij shifts within stanzas between the past and present tenses, creating thereby temporal intersections that parallel the spatial intersections found in a number of his lyrics. The equation with Puškin's poem "Mednyj vsadnik" ("The Bronze Horseman"), implied by

Annenskij's title, is brought home here by a statue that, like the statue of Peter the Great in Puškin's work, has come to life. Annenskij's blurring of time further stresses the tie between the two statues.   Puškin intended for his horseman to symbolize St. Petersburg and, by extension, the power of the state as embodied in the Western-oriented tsar.   Annenskij's sculpture stands for St. Petersburg as well.   It is equated with the power of art as emblemized by Puškin.   Equally significant, the statue stands for the three-dimensional visual image, an image given even greater power by its sudden animation.   The enduring quality of this art is in sharp contrast to the fragile music of the next lyric.

In contrast to "Bronzovyj poèt" ("The Bronze Poet"), "Posle koncerta" ("After the Concert") emphasizes the vulnerability of art, but the art Annenskij regards as fragile is music, not sculpture, and music is generally equated with torment in his work.

"Posle koncerta"

"V alleju černye spustilis' nebesa,
No serdcu v ètu noč' ne prevozmoč' ustalost'. . .
Pogasšie ogni, nemye golosa, -
Neužto èto vsë, čto ot mečty ostalos'?

O, kak pečalen byl odežd ee atlas,
I vyrez žutko bel sredi naplečij černyx!
Kak žalko bylo mne ee nedvižnyx glaz
I snežnoj lajki ruk, molitvenno-pokornyx!

A skol'ko bylo tam razvejano duši
Sredi rassejannyx, mjatežnyx i bessleznyx!
Čto zvukov prolito, vzlelejannyx v tiši,
Sirenevyx, i laskovyx, i zvëzdnyx!

Tak s niti porvannoj v volnen'i inogda,
Sred' mesjačnyx lučej, i nežny i ognisty,
V rosistuju travu katjatsja ametisty
I gibnut bez sleda."[23]

"The black skies have descended onto the garden path,
But on this night the heart cannot overcome weariness. . .
The lights have gone out, the voices are dumb, -
Is this really all that has remained from a dream?

Oh, how sad was the satin of her clothes,
And [her] décolletage was frighteningly white against
The black shoulder straps!

How I pitied her immobile eyes
And her suppliant-submissive hands in snowy kidskin!
And how much of [her] soul was scattered there
Among the dispersed, the restless, and the tearless!
What sounds were spilled, nurtured in silence,
Lilac-colored, and tender, and starry!
Thus at times amethysts, in the tender and fiery moonlight,
Roll into the dewy grass
From a thread broken in agitation,
And perish without a trace."

Annenskij's singer is a "portrait" in black and white, favored tones of the art-nouveau period (used, for example, by Beardsley and Whistler). Her black dress sets off the whiteness of her skin, with the weakness of her pale skin underscored by her motionless eyes and submissive hands, hands clad in white gloves that echo her pallor. Her hands and eyes, outlets for her personality, are mute. Her fragility is the fragility of sound.

The "starry, tender, lilac-colored sounds" of the third stanza symbolize the beauty of her performance, lilac generally being equated in Annenskij's work with unreality. Lilac in addition suggests a world of diffused light in which conventional time has disappeared,[24] a state echoed by the word "zvëzdnyj" ("starry"), which also implies separation from everyday time. The ephemerality of music is again symbolized in the last stanza by the amethysts, which sparkled briefly before disappearing in the grass. The crystalline structure of the amethysts, like the crystals and straight lines of the lyrics discussed above, stands for the formal beauty of art which can fall prey to time. Here that art is identified with music and, more specifically, with the sound orientation of Symbolism. It is an art that does not endure, in contrast to the concrete world of the plastic arts found in "Bronzovyj poèt" ("The Bronze Poet").

In "Poèzija" ("Poetry"), art transcends the everyday world and allows the poet unlimited access into a realm of absolute beauty.

"Nad vys'ju plamennoj Sinaja
Ljubit' tuman Ee lučej,
Molit'sja Ej, Ee ne znaja,

Tem beznadežno gorjačej,
No iz lazuri fimiama,
Ot lilij prazdnogo venca,
Bežat'. . .prezrev gordynju xrama
I slavoslovie žreca,

Čtob v okeane mutnyx dalej,
V bezumnom čajan'i svjatyn',
Iskat' sledov Ee sandalij
Meždu zanosami pustyn'.ʺ[25]

"Poetry"

"Above the flaming height of Sinai
It is all the more hopelessly ardent
To love the mist of Her rays,
To entreat Her, not knowing Her.

But to run. . .having disdained the arrogance of the temple
And the glorification of the priest,
From the azure of incense,
From the lilies of the useless crown,

In order to seek the traces of Her sandals
Among the sand drifts of the desert,
In the ocean of turbid distances,
In the mad expectation of sacred things."

The setting is the Sinai, site of the testing of faith and of Biblical miracles. The word "height" ("vys'") refers to the mountainous terrain of the south of the Sinai, perhaps to Mt. Sinai itself; it also elevates the area spiritually by placing it nearer the sky, the source of inspiration. "Plamennyj" ("flaming") not only describes the concentrated heat of the desert, but carries in addition the religious connotation of the fire that can purge sin and memory (as in the Burning Bush, or in Puškin's poem "Prorok," "The Prophet," to which this lyric bears a strong resemblance).[26] The sandals of the last stanza underscore the heat of the desert and were the footgear of assorted Biblical personages.

The Sinai figured in the Bible, and it has traditionally been the goal for pilgrims who wished to renounce their previously worldly lives and the decadence of society.[27] This was especially true for the Orthodox, for whom Rome had no such significance. The desert as a haven of religious contemplation and an escape from the sins of society, specifically the city, figures in the second stanza, with the first line containing the phrase "lazur' fimiama" ("azure of incense").[28] Along with the lilies of the second line, incense suggests funerals and Orthodox ritual; both incense and the lilies mark the spiritual decay of the established religion from which the poet is escaping. This established religion may well be the mysticism of later Symbolism, with the incense and lilies standing for the lack of clarity characterizing this movement. Poetry is contrasted to the vision of Sophia that Solov'ev saw in Egypt, which may well figure in Annenskij's choice of this poetic "setting." The poem as a whole almost certainly represents Annenskij's escape from a burdensome, "official" school of poetry in his quest for clear art. While the urban religious world may symbolize the society from which the poet has escaped, it might also stand for the world of dogmatic literary schools. The poet has fled to the purity and isolation of the desert to await the furtive appearances of Poetry.

Annenskij translates spatial terms into poetic inspiration in stanza three. The poet exists in an "ocean of turbid distances," in the "mad expectation of sacred things." The ocean corresponds to the infinity of unlimited space and time into which the sandals of Poetry have intruded with a sharp definiteness. Annenskij has personified Poetry in the last stanza, where he speaks of the "traces of Her sandals." The narrator, who receives only indications (signs) that Poetry has been in a particular place, never sees Her directly. He further mentions the "mist of Her rays" and "praying to Her" ("entreating Her"), although not "knowing Her." The remoteness of Poetry suggests that the poet sees merely a hint of a larger, universally significant symmetry, a hint he can transform into poetry. The symmetry corresponds to the lines and crystals of other lyrics, a visual symmetry of planed constructions anticipating the later Constructivism of such avant-garde artists as Vladimir Tatlin and Naum Gabo. It is a utilization of art to control and delimit space, and it is this very shaping of space that will figure in the essays and poetry of Mandel'štam.

Annenskij's combination of religious imagery with aesthetic symbols reaches a climax in this stanza, particularly in his employment of images suggesting the diffusion of light. The light of the desert represents inspiration and provides a backdrop for the poet's own formulation of the signs of beauty that he perceives. "Poèzija" can therefore be considered a poem about the visualization of poetic inspiration and its transformation into art.

The visual images of "Poèzija" are contrasted to music in "Smyčok i struny" ("The Bow and Strings"), which recounts the torment involved in creating a work of art.

"Kakoj tjaželyj, temnyj bred!
Kak èti vysi mutno-lunny!
Kasat'sja skripki stol'ko let
I ne uznat' pri svete struny!

Komu ž nas nado? Kto zažeg
Dva želtyx lika, dva unylyx. . .
I vdrug počuvstvoval smyčok,
Čto kto-to vzjal i kto-to slil ix.

'O kak davno! Skvoz' ètu t'mu
Skaži odno: ty ta li, ta li?'
I struny lastilis' k nemu,
Zvenja, no lastjas', trepetali.

'Ne pravda l', bol'še nikogda
My ne rasstanemsja? dovol'no? . .'
I skripka otvečala *da*,
No serdcu skripki bylo bol'no.

Smyčok vsë ponjal, on zatix,
A v skripke èxo vsë deržalos'. . .
I bylo mukoju dlja nix,
Čto ljudjam muzykoj kazalos'.

No čelovek ne pogasil
Do utra sveč. . .I struny peli. . .
Liš' solnce ix našlo bez sil
Na černom barxate posteli."[29]

"What a heavy, dark delirium!
How turbidly-moonlit are these heights!
To touch the violin for so many years
And not to recognize the strings in the light!

Who needs us? Who has lit
Two yellow faces, two despondent ones. . .
And suddenly the bow sensed
That someone took and someone merged them.

'Oh, how long! Through this darkness
Say only: art thou the same one, the same one?'
And the strings caressed him,

Ringing, but caressing, trembled.

'Is it not true, we will never
Part again? Is that right?. . .
And the violin answered *yes*,
But the heart of the violin was aching.

The bow understood everything, he fell silent,
But the echo still held in the violin. . .
And what was agony for them,
Seemed music to people.

But the man did not extinguish
The candles until morning. . .And the strings sang. . .
Only the sun found them without strength
On the black velvet of the bed."

While "Smyčok i struny" can be interpreted on one level as a love poem,[30] it is almost certainly about the process of artistic creation.   The creative state here is an abnormal one, symbolized by the "yellow faces" of the candle flames, a recurrent, nightmarish image in Annenskij's lyrics, and by the phrase "kakoj tjaželyj, tëmnyj bred!" ("What a heavy, dark delirium").   The "delirium" is linked with the "heights" of the second line, both suggesting that the creative act is like a mystical union with a higher being, the essence of Symbolism.   The conception of artistic creativity as an act involving mystical union is re-emphasized when the narrator states that someone picked up the violin and bow and "merged them" ("slil ix"), the verb "slit'" ("to merge") implying a flowing together synonymous with the mystical state.

The distortion, even absence, of visual images is suggested not only by the odd appearance of the candle flames, but also by the word "t'ma" ("darkness").   The bow and strings are placed on the "black velvet" of the bed, black symbolizing the absence of light and velvet emphasizing the tactile perception of the unseeing state. The bow and strings know each other only through the torment of touch.

The realization that their union is to be brief brings grief to the bow and strings, but their pain is apprehended as music (art) by the listener.   This can be seen in the third stanza from the words "ty ta li, ta li" ("Art thou the same one, the same one"), which contain a variety of back and front vowels that suggest different musical tones produced by the violin.

Annenskij is almost certainly speaking about the later, mystical Symbolists in this lyric. In their emphasis of sound over visual stimulae, their conception of creation as a tormenting mystical union, and their orientation toward the unconscious mind, the later Symbolists resemble the bow and strings of "Smyčok i struny" rather than the novice in the Sinai in "Poèzija" ("Poetry").

Time occupies a place of supreme importance in Annenskij's poetry, for it is the regulator of the days and seasons, the ruler of life. Time connects all of Annenskij's other themes, providing a focal point for understanding his view of the material world and his emphasis on art. His stress on temporality is closely linked to the theories of the Acmeists. He presents time in two guises: as an intellectual conception and as an external force. "Stal'naja cikada" ("The Steel Cicada") exemplifies time as mental invention.

"Ja znal, čto ona vernetsja
I budet so mnoj - Toska.
Zvjaknet i zapaxnetsja
S dver'ju časovščika. . .

Serdca stal'nogo trepet
So strekotan'em kryl
Scepit i vnov' rascepit
Tot, kto ej dver' otkryl. . .

Žadnym krylom cikady
Neterpelivo b'jut;
Sčast'ju l', čto blizko, rady,
Muki l' konec zovut? . .

Stol'ko skazat' im nado,
Tak daleko ujti. . .
Rozno, uvy! cikada,
Naši ležat puti.

Zdes' my s toboj liš' čudo,
Žit' nam s toboju teper'
Tol'ko minutu - pokuda
Ne raspaxnulas' dver'. . .

Zvjaknet i zapaxnetsja,
I budeš' ty tak daleka. . .
Molča sejčas vernetsja
I budet so mnoj - Toska."[31]

"I knew that she would return
And be with me – Anguish.
She will twinkle and wrap herself
With the watchmaker's door. . .
He who opened the door for her
Will link and again unlink
The palpitation of the steel heart
With the trembling of wings. . .
The cicadas beat impatiently
With an eager wing;
Are they glad of the happiness that is close,
Or are they summoning the end of torment? . . .
There is so much one must say to them,
It is so far to go. . .
Alas! cicada,
Our paths lie apart.
Here thou and I are only a miracle
For me to live with thee now
Only a minute remains
Until the door has been thrown open. . .
It will twinkle and shut,
And thou wiltt be so far away. . .
Anguish will silently return soon
And will be with me."

"The Steel Cicada" is an unusually complex lyric, with such images as beating wings (here of the cicada), "toska" ("anguish"), and the double persona ("thou and I") found in several of Annenskij's other poems.   If anguish can be considered a static state, then it is juxtaposed to the frenetic activity of the cicadas, symbols of time.   Annenskij is not content merely to suggest the presence of time, but in fact speeds up the tempo in the course of the poem, offering in this way the greatest possible contrast between the motion of time and the constancy of anguish.   He uses the adverb "neterpelivo" ("impatiently") to demonstrate that the emotional state of the cicada, never strictly defined, is constantly changing; this change implies the sudden passage of time.   Annenskij also employs short phrases with enjambement to achieve a staccato effect.   The expression "Stol'ko skazat' im nado" (alternatively translated as "There is so much they need to say" or "There is so much to say to them") crams a great deal of activity into a very short period of time. The exclamation point after "Uvy!" ("Alas!") provides another sudden break that speeds up time. From this climax until the end of the poem, the excitement gradually subsides and the action slows down. Having been caught up in time in the middle stanzas, the persona has once again moved outside it. The anguish that haunted the persona in the first stanza returns again in the last one, and he has become reconciled to its presence, recognizing that his companionship with the cicada is a "čudo" ("miracle") that will last only for a minute. The pain of separation here recalls the suffering of the persona and his alter ego in "Dvojnik" ("The Double") and of the violin and bow in "Smyčok i struny" ("The Bow and Strings"), both lyrics having been discussed above. In stanza six time is stopped, for the lid will snap and the cicada will then be far away. The sudden disappearance of the cicada may imply that one's involvement in a cycle of events makes time exist only in the present; the moment that has passed is already beyond recall, i.e., distant.

The silent return of anguish fills the vacuum left by the disappearance of time, and her existence outside time is symbolized by the adverb "molča" ("silently"), silence implying lack of action, timelessness. If the cicada and, in turn, the watch, stand for the power of the mind to organize, and, by extension, to control existence, then the re-emergence of anguish points to the failure of that effort.

"Nocturno" shows time as an external force.

"Temnuju vyberi noč' i v pole, bezljudnom i golom,
V mrak okunis'. . .pust' veter, provejas', utixnet,
Pust' v nebe xolodnom tusklye zvezdy, migaja,
zadremljut. . .
Serdcu skaži, čtob udarov ono ne sčitalo. . .
Šag zaderži i prislušajsja! Ty ne odin. . .
Točno kryl'ja
Pticy, namokšie tjažko, plyvut sred' tumana.
Slušaj. . .èto letit xiščnaja, vlastnaja ptica,
Vremja tu pticu zovut, i na kryl'jax u nej tvoja
sila,
Radosti son mimoletnyj, nadežd zolotye loxmot'ja. . ."[32]

"Choose a dark night in a field, deserted and bare,
Plunge into the gloom. . .let the wind, winnowing, die away,
Let the dim stars in the cold sky, twinkling,
doze off. . .
Tell (thy) heart, that it should not count its beats. . .
Hold thy step and listen! Thou art not alone. . .It is as if
the wings
Of a bird, heavily soaked, are swimming through the mist.
Listen. . .it is a predatory, powerful bird flying,
That bird is called *Time*, and on its wings is thy
strength,
The fleeting dream of joy, the golden rags of hopes. . .

The windless, nocturnal field expands space and stops time.
There is no motion or process that would serve to measure it, for
the twinkling of the stars is so remote that it represents eternity.
An element of mystery and anticipation is introduced with the
words "Ty ne odin. . ." ("Thou art not alone. . ."), and the wings
of an unseen and therefore mysterious bird sweep down. To
emphasize the significance and force of this bird, akin to other
prophetic, powerful birds in his work, Annenskij gives it weight.
The bird has been swimming through mist, and its wings are
heavy with wetness.

Having established the weakness of the persona relative to the
bird, the narrator further reveals that this rapacious bird is called
time. The details of the last line further define the impotence of
the persona and add a note of bitter frustration. The dream of
joy is fleeting; the hopes of life are only golden rags after the
ravages of time. Life is defined in terms of the future but
simultaneously controlled and ultimately destroyed by time. Life is
without substance, dream is impermanent, and both are impotent
before the all-consuming might of time.

By dividing Annenskij's lyrics according to six major themes,
we have been able to determine the connection between his world
view and poetic practice. All six are interrelated, for nature is an
external reflection of life simultaneously representing beauty, while
the dream is life's unconscious reflection and a temporary
counterpart of death. Both life and death are specific points on
the continuum of time that is an intellectual counterpart to the
band of visible light produced by the prism-poet, an image that

will be further investigated in Chapter Three.   Time and poetry
emerge in the end as the dominant themes.

Time is process and final disintegration, tying together life,
nature and death, while life is the temporary immersion in this
process. It is the poet's realization of the frustrating uselessness of
temporality that produces the psychological state known as "toska"
("yearning," "anguish," "ennui"), "toska" being a constant
awareness of the limits of existence.   Annenskij's reiteration of
"toska" is a rejection of mysticism and underscores the enormous
gulf separating him from the later Symbolists.

Nature provides the illusion of permanence and constancy for
which the persona yearns, but its final impotence (the melting
crystals) produces both bitterness at this enormous disappointment
and a sense of futility.   Dream is a means of evading time, with a
possibility of escaping from the conscious awareness of process into
a world with neither change nor motion, a lifeless world.   But its
lifeless, unconscious   state is no reasonable alternative to the
inexorability of time.

Death signifies both total subservience to time and final
escape from it, and can be regarded as the last of a long chain of
processes defining life. As the end of the process of life, death can
provide deliverance from time, but in this escape one leaves life
behind.   Death is the final negation of consciousness, a symbol of a
total and a permanent timelessness.

Annenskij allows only poetry, a poetry related to the visual
world, to escape from the clutches of time.   Produced by a union
between the artist and the creative spirit ("Poetry," the muse), art
provides a loophole by allowing the artist to endure through the
beauty he has created.   (It is precisely for this reason that music,
the art of process, is excluded from permanence.)   Since art is not
subject to the laws of time, it can be seen as transcending them.[33]
The statue of Puškin in "Bronzovyj poèt" ("The Bronze Poet") is
Annenskij's most potent symbol for the longevity of art, and it is
with sculpture that he has made his statement.

Annenskij's determination that time is the ruling force, a
powerful symbol for process and, eventually, death contrasts sharply
with the aesthetic values and poetic practice of the Symbolists,
who sought to escape from the temporal, physical world.   For
Annenskij, acceptance of time emphasizes acceptance of the "three
dimensions of existence" found in the Acmeists' doctrine.   His
aesthetic hypothesis that the creation of a work of (specifically,

visual) art transcends time is linked to Mandel'štam's conviction that art, exemplified by architectural monuments and the plastic arts and characterized by conscious construction, endures in spite of time and circumstance.

CHAPTER THREE

DEVICES IN ANNENSKIJ'S VERSE

Annenskij's acceptance of the limitations of the physical world, as demonstrated by his emphasis on time and use of visual images, is paralleled by an employment of poetic devices that achieve much the same effect stylistically. His generous utilization particularly of personification and concretizing devices lends a sense of solidity and definiteness to his poems. His reliance, in addition, on conversational devices enables the critic to establish a tie between his work and the prose of his period, specifically, the short stories of Čexov. The resemblance between Annenskij's personas and some of Čexov's characters is striking. This similarity demonstrates Annenskij's linkage with the prose writing immediately preceding and contemporaneous with his work, in contradistinction to the schism between the Symbolists and their immediate forebears.

Because Annenskij tended to favor concrete, distinct objects as poetic images, his verse differed markedly from the abstractness characterizing the work of his contemporaries. For the later Symbolists, concrete objects represented the earthly ties from which they were attempting to escape, while abstraction signified mystical retreat. Annenskij's preference for the definite and concrete would find a later expression in the essays of the Acmeists. Because of this similarity, an analysis of his use of such devices will constitute the focal point of this chapter.

Annenskij employed personification to humanize nature and inanimate objects,[1] thereby establishing a link between the persona and his physical surroundings, a link reflecting his emphasis on structural and pictorial qualities. In a similar manner, his comparison of the seasons of the year with the stages in a person's life demonstrates this thematically.[2] Annenskij's specific devices for personification are capitalization, simile, metaphor, and apostrophe. They will be discussed in the order given.

In Russian, as well as English, capitalization is reserved for proper nouns, usually for persons' names, and Annenskij's use of capitalization is an anthropomorphizing device. "Den'" ("Day") in the lyric "Toska vozvrata" ("The Anguish of Return") is languishing, "His sin unprayed for. . ." ("Svoim grexom neotmolennym/ Tomitsja Den' perežitoj. . .")[3] The reluctance of Day to say his prayers (which are associated here with the approach of evening, or with dying) stresses the equation between the approaching night and death. The consequent humanizing implied by capitalization is emphasized by the human emotions, fear or hesitation, that Day displays.

Annenskij capitalizes "Užas" ("Terror") and "Strax" ("Fear") in "Pered panixidoj" ("Before the Requiem"), where "Užas" is reflected in white mirrors, in stanza three, at the requiem service ("Liš' Užas v belyx zerkalax").[4] If "white" signifies nothingness, the void, lifelessness, and the mirror is a poor reflection of life, then the related capitalization and resultant personification of "Terror" personify the horror of death. The mirror, too, symbolizes a world once removed, an optical correspondence to the "other side" of existence.

"Strax" ("Fear"), with a bow, distributes candles to the mourners ("nam" or "us"): "I s pojasnym poklonom Strax/ Nam sveči razdaet." Candles are commonly used in Russian Orthodox services, particularly during the Easter worship and the services for the dead, with the flame signifying the triumph of the soul over death. By changing "Fear" into the priest's assistant distributing the lighted candles, Annenskij underscores the horror of death and the terror of the mourners. The candle flames here, like the lights in "Smyčok i struny" ("The Bow and Strings") and the artificial or weakened light in other poems, is distorted, frightening and, in the end, pessimistic. The poem as a whole expresses the persona's conception of death as a malevolent force bent on personal destruction, and the use of capitalization and concomitant personification turns this lyric into a little dramatic scene and emphasizes the inescapable force of reality.

Annenskij capitalizes "Toska" ("Anguish") in several poems, including "Stal'naja cikada" ("The Steel Cicada"), discussed in the second chapter. "Toska" also appears in "Moja Toska" ("My Anguish"), where Annenskij has endowed it with the personality of a stock character in literature, the insidious woman who fastens herself upon a man and then ruins him. Representing the unhappiness that has poisoned the poet's life, "Toska" alone will survive him. ("Vse budet žit' moe, odna moja Toska. . .")[5] For Annenskij, "Toska" assumes special significance as a concrete symbol for life, a distillation of life into visual, even physical form.

In addition to capitalization, Annenskij uses the simile to identify abstract concepts and inaminate objects with human beings. In line three of "Maki" ("The Poppies"), the poppies are compared with lips "full of temptations and poisons." ("Vsë maki . . ./Kak guby, polnye soblazna i otrav.")[6] Red lips are alluring, with extreme sexual attractiveness having an overtone of danger ("full of poisons"). Poppies are also the source of opium, a "temptation and poison." In the second stanza, poppies that have dried out are compared with the heads of old women. ("I maki soxlye, kak golovy starux"). Having lost their malignant brightness, they now have their weary heads bowed like those of old women close to death, stressing once again Annenskij's equation of the cycles of human life with the stages in nature. As with his use of "toska," Annenskij has again made life an unappealing alternative. The poem as a whole is like a "vanitas" with flowers, demonstrating once again Annenskij's link with painting, specifically with Western Baroque art; he must surely have been exposed to such works while travelling in Italy.

"Probuždenie" ("The Awakening") is personified through simile. In the third stanza, the sun is shining through the mist, "yellow," like a "sick man who has [just] gotten up." ("Solnce. . . /Želto, kak vstavšij bol'noj.")[7] Two comparisons are at work here. Perhaps the sun, equated with an invalid, seems ill because it has just risen out of darkness and night (symbolic of death) into the daylight (life), and, like the persona, is in limbo. The "sick" man is identified with a depressing life devoid of significance or hope, evoking once again the image of Toska, or anguish, that haunts Annenskij's lyrics. Like personification, the simile too renders the general specific, the abstract concrete, placing the lyrics in which it occurs firmly within the confines of the physical world. The light of the "sickly" sun, typical of the pallid light that barely illumines the world of his verse, underscores his pessimism, touched on above. It is a pessimism caused by his awareness of time and emphasizes his acceptance of his place within the three-dimensional world.

Annenskij employs the metaphor for personification more frequently than any other device; the use of the instrumental case provides an elegant means of doing this. In "Staraja šarmanka"

("The Old Barrel Organ"), stubborn winter bares its teeth like a beast. ("I, oščerjas, zverem otstupila/ Za aprel' uprjamaja zima.")[8] Later, its helmet pulled down over its brows, it is ready for continued battle. ("Už opjat' na brovi šlem nadvinut"). Annenskij has not only stressed the ferocity of winter through this metaphor, but has again emphasized the link between man and the natural world. A similar comparison occurs in stanza three, where an open window looks down onto the grass in the street ("I gljadit raskrytoe okno"), and is therefore identified with consciousness, i.e., a person. The principal metaphors in the poem center around the transformation of the barrel organ into a street musician. Shivering with cold, the barrel organ suffers the poverty of the musician and is equated here, on one level, with society's rejection of the artist. ("Liš' šarmanku staruju znobit") In the last stanza, it continues to play in spite of the torment of creativity. ("razve b pet', kružas', on perestal / Ottogo, čto pet' nel'zja, ne mučas'? . .") The barrel organ is related to the singer of "Posle koncerta" ("After the Concert") and the bow and strings of "Smyčok i struny" ("The Bow and Strings"), all of whom/which are equated with the artist who suffers while creating. Again, this suffering is related to *music*, not the plastic arts, and music is associated with temporality, with art that cannot endure. There is a further link between the musician and the Symbolists, particularly the later ones, for it was these poets who reduced poetry to sound, causing thereby a juncture in the visual orientation that was vital to the poetry preceding and following them.

This equation of music and suffering is developed further in "Vtoroj fortep'jannyj sonet" ("The Second Piano Sonnet"). In the first stanza, the fingers of the pianist are dancing slave girls ("Nad rižoj beloju, kak ugol' volosa,/ Rjadami strojnymi nevol'nicy pljasali.")[9] The metaphor is extended in stanza two, where greedy wasps have exhausted the dancers. ("I osy žadnye pljasunij donimali") By comparing the fingers to dancers, Annenskij has equated music with the dance, the equivalent of music in motion, a form of animate sculpture.[10] That the dancers are slaves stung by wasps echoes yet again the connection between music and suffering made in such lyrics as "Smyčok i struny" ("The Bow and Strings"), "Staraja šarmanka" ("The Old Barrel Organ"), and "Posle koncerta" ("After the concert").[11] The greedy wasps are the "sting of time" fatal to music and the arts associated with it, art unable to endure because it is not visual. Annenskij has again stressed the limitations of Symbolist verse, which relies upon aural, not visual images.

In "Veter" ("The Wind"), the wind is named only in the title, but the poem as a whole is a catalogue of its activities. The wind is "angry" and draws a veil across a field of rye. (". . . serdit,/ On pole rži zadernet flёrom"). During the summer, it furrows the wave in the lakes (". . .nežnym lёtom borozdit/ Volnu po rozovym ozeram") and threatens ships at sea and tangles the sails (". . .grozit on korablju/ I parusa svivaet v žgut'ja").[12] The wind is an ideal tenor for a personifying metaphor, because the movement it causes is identified with animation and it seems to display emotions. It is reduced additionally to the visual effects it produces. Annenskij's equation of man with nature, like his use of concrete objects and emphasis on visual images, is a facet of his acceptance of the physical world.

The rain of "Oktjabr'skij mif" ("The October Myth") is a blind man walking around on the roof. ("Ja šagi slepogo slyšu:/ Nado mnoju on vsju nočʹ/ Ostupaetsja o kryšu.")[13] This metaphor is deliberately confused in the second stanza, where the poet does not know if his own tears are contracting his heart, or if these are the tears of the blind man (the rain). ("I moi lʹ, ne znaju, žgut/ Serdce slezy, ili èto/ Te, kotorye begut/ U slepogo bez otveta.") As in the previous poem and with a similar motive on the part of the poet, nature is both an extension and a reflection of human emotions; here, tears have become rain in the natural world. There is also the link between flowing water (rain or tears) and sorrow, symbols of temporal destruction juxtaposed to the crystalline, planer structures of winter's ice. Because crystals are equated with beauty, their loss to time is a tragic motif for Annenskij.

The moon is grinding a knife in the grass in "Za ogradoj" ("Beyond the Fence"), and is even given the power of speech. ("Mesjac v travax točit nož./ Mesjac vidit, mesjac skažet: Ubežišʹ. . .da ne ujdešʹ. . .'")[14] The moon as a threatening figure represents the terrors of night, the nightmare and, ultimately, death. The fence stands for the boundaries of the "civilized," "safe" world, while the pale light is terrifying, resembling the weak or reflected light in other lyrics dealt with earlier. Nature is also personified in "Listy" ("The Leaves"), where the leaves circling above the dust symbolize nature dying in the fall, a common conceit in the poetry of Baratynskij, Fet, and Annenskij.

("Kružatsja nežnye listy/ I ne xotjat kosnutsja praxa. . .")[15] The animated leaves are like the wind in "Veter" ("The Wind"), identified with man and infused with human emotions. Again, this link between the human and natural both anthropomorphizes nature and places man firmly within the context of the visible, physical world.

Annenskij personifies Midnight in "Zimnij poezd" ("The Winter Train"), using metaphor to compare it with a monk carrying a broken lantern through the coaches of a moving train. ("Proxodit Polnoč' po vagonam./ Ona - kak prizračnyj monax.")[16] Annenskij's monk is strongly reminiscent of the monk in Čexov's famous story, "Černyj monax" ("The Black Monk"), a mad vision that destroys the protagonist. Annenskij's link with Čexov can be seen clearly in this lyric. Annenskij often rode the commuter train to and from his post at the lyceum in Tsarskoe Selo, and it is not surprising that a train should have intruded into his work. The journey here is a common symbol for life, while the intrusion of the black monk clearly stands for nightmare and, ultimately, death. Annenskij has motion within motion, a moving figure on a moving train, causing further loss of orientation. In sharp contrast to Symbolist poetic practice focusing on the use of abstractions, Annenskij has instead made the abstract concrete in this poem.

In addition to employing capitalization, simile, and metaphor for personification and concretization, Annenskij also uses apostrophe, addressing an object in the second person singular as if it were human. "Ty opjat' so mnoj" ("Thou Art Again with Me") contains an apostrophe in the title as well as in the body of the poem. "Ty" ("Thou") is autumn, and is the poet's friend ("podruga") as well.[17] The familiarity inherent in "ty" and in "podruga" implies that autumn is probably the persona's alter ego as well as his friend, underscoring once more the link between man and nature. Because autumn is the season identified with the death of nature associated with the approach of winter, the relationship of autumn to winter is like that between illness and death. It is understandable that Annenskij, who suffered for years from the heart disease that eventually killed him, should have identified himself with autumn. The abstract has been made concrete.

Annenskij also uses apostrophe in "Toska sada" ("The Anguish of the Garden"), in which the persona says that he cannot love as freely as "thou," an unnamed auditor.[18] "Ty" could refer alternatively to anguish, the garden, a woman, or even the muse. The poem on one level is about love, and Annenskij has used nature, symbolized here by the garden, as an extension of human emotions and an emblem of the union of man and nature, a tamed form of nature. In addition, the garden is a living construction, architecture as applied to nature, representing man's shaping of space and the world outside himself. It is therefore related to planed constructions, the concrete visual images of the poet, linking man firmly with actuality as the Acmeists would later do.

Annenskij employs personification, through capitalization, simile, and metaphor, as a corollary to concretization, which can be defined as the use of any literary devices rendering the general specific and the abstract concrete. Both personification and concretization signify an acceptance of the confines of the three-dimensional world, an antithesis of the Symbolists' view. Annenskij tended not only to concretize abstractions, but also to rely heavily on the use of ordinary objects.[19] In "U groba" ("At the Grave"), containing a description of the apartment of a man who has recently died, Annenskij compares his "forgotten" piano with a horse in a horsecloth. ("Kak kon' poponoju, odet rojal' zabytyj.")[20] Just as the riderless horse symbolizes the fallen warrior, so does the covered piano signify the instrument without the musician, art without the artist. Again, music is the art form linked with temporality, contrasted to the enduring qualities of the visual image, the plastic arts.

In "Zaveščanie" ("The Legacy"), a singer on a ship is compared with a bird. ("A esli pet' - tak pticej poj/ Svobodno, zvonko, smelo.")[21] Singing here symbolizes poetry, but the emphasis is on clarity and, by extension, on form. Like "Poètu" ("To the Poet"), this lyric is an instruction, a "legacy," from an older, more experienced poet to a younger one. The bird's singing is "free" ("svobodno"), with "free" emphasized by "resonantly" ("zvonko") and "boldly" ("smelo"). Resonance is loudness with depth, boldness implying dynamics and range of tone. All three define a work of art skillfully composed without being facile, a work in which structure is emphasized.

The identification of the bird with singing implies the flight of song, for song is airborne and consists, in scientific terms, of vibrations in the air. "Freely" and "boldly" also suggest the sweeping motion of flight and, by extension, the bird. Through singing and flight, the bird has become the concrete representation of art, an art that can transcend (soar above the earth) through the beauty of its form, or structure.

A simile is the concretizing medium in "Poslednie sireni" ("The Last Lilacs"), in which the poet compares his breast (heart) with a storm cloud. ("Segodnja grud' moja želanija polna,/ Kak tuča, polnaja i groma i sverkanij.") The poem as a whole deals with the persona's relationship with a woman, a relationship evidently marred by misunderstanding. The garden setting represents the heart of the persona, who is pained by his awareness that affection is nearly gone. Again, the garden is a structured, natural setting serving as an extension of the psyche. His love is symbolized by the lilacs of the title, fragile flowers of a pastel hue linked in his verse with ephemerality, specifically with the transitoriness of emotion.[22] The poem is firmly set within the visual world, the world of structured nature, and, again, man and nature are one.

The heaviness of the cloud in stanza three underscores the oppressive weight of the persona's desire. Thunder and the lightning flashes in the clouds symbolize the rapid fluctuations and enormous strength of emotions, both nature and emotions having equal power to eclipse other forces. The dark gray of the storm cloud ("tuča"), in contrast to the usual whiteness of the fair-weather cloud ("oblako"), denotes an absence of light and emphasizes the persona's despair. Again, Annenskij has relied on color, a visual symbol, to express emotion. Annenskij draws further comparisons between the heavy cloud, full of rain, and the heart heavy with emotion, with tears. Clouds in addition represent the boundary between earthly existence and a vision of the infinite. The heavy cloud has completely blotted out infinity by hiding the sky from view and, as a result, has caused the persona to limit his world to an immediate emotional crisis, an effect also produced by the onerous pressure of a negative emotion. If a clear sky is linked with light, specifically, with rays of light and with clarity, then heavy clouds stand for obscurity, darkness, and depression; by extension they symbolize the unnamed "Toska," "Anguish."

"Zabvenie" ("Oblivion") contains a complex simile in which "oblivion" is compared initially with an autumn day ("I zabven'e, no zabven'e,/ Kak osennij mjagkij den'.")[23] It is subsequently identified with the midday sun in the temple. ("Kak poludnja solnce v xrame/ Skvoz' uzor stekla cvetnoj. - ") Only the vehicle of the simile is given. Oblivion is compared not so much with the autumn day itself as with the diffused light of autumn. Suspended in the dust of decaying leaves, the autumn light passes through the dust, and similarly the sunlight in the temple shines through the stained glass and acquires its colors. The diffusion of light suspends clarity and makes the passage of time difficult to detect, creating the state known as oblivion, a state outside time.

The light passing through the colored pattern of the glass can be seen further as the inspiration of the poet, passing through him to create art. Typically, Annenskij depicts inspiration visually. The equation of refracted light with poetry will also inform "V volšebnuju prizmu" ("Into the Magic Prism"), to be discussed below. The state of oblivion caused by the light is symbolic of art's mastery over time, the thrust of "Bronzovyj poèt" ("The Bronze Poet"), treated in the preceding chapter.

"V volšebnuju prizmu" ("Into the Magic Prism") is a metapoem related to the lyric discussed above. In the last two lines, Annenskij asserts that there "is not a more victorious rainbow,/ Than the rainbow of final torments! . ."[24] ("No radugi netu pobednej/, Čem raduga končennyx muk! . .") The rainbow has Old Testament connotations as a symbol of hope, an end to suffering, and therefore it stands for the future. In "V volšebnuju prizmu," the poet is symbolized by the prism he holds, with art providing hope and the rainbow resulting from the light bent in the prism. The rainbow can be considered constructed light. The poet absorbs the ray of light (inspiration) and transforms it into a rainbow (the beauty of a poem, symbolized by transformed light). The torments to which Annenskij refers may be those experienced by the poet while creating art. The rainbow signifies the end of torment (the creative act). Annenskij's connection of poetic creation with light and color rather than sound is in keeping with his emphasis on rays of light, planes, and visual structure (including the gardens of the poems discussed above).

Annenskij concretizes the sunset in "Maj" ("May"), remarking in the first stanza that the "dim glass shines with the fire of the west." ("I tol'ko tuskloe steklo/ Požarom zapada blistaet.")[25] He has produced not only a visual image, but a concrete, solid one as well, one with planar structure. The "glass" of the evening sky is contrasted to the fire of the sunset. "Fire" and "glass" anthopomorphize the sky, making it an extension of the human world; this lyric is therefore linked with the garden poems discussed above.

By employing synaesthesia, Annenskij is able to jar the customary world of the reader, "solidifying" the image by enclosing it within the intersecting planes of two types of perception.[26]   In the first stanza of "Toska miraža" ("The Anguish of the Mirage"), the "last color [of sunset] went out,/ Like the whisper in a midnight prayer. . ." ("Pogasla poslednjaja kraska,/ Kak šepot v polnočnoj mol'be. . .")[27]   Since whisper is speech on the threshold of audibility, the comparison of the sunset to a whisper suggests minimal visibility.   The phrase "midnight prayer" links the whisper with night, but the additional connection of the whisper with sunset marks the approach of evening.   Annenskij has telescoped time, erasing the hours between sundown and midnight; he has incorporated it within the scope of the senses.   In so doing, having made time palpable, he has humanized it.

Annenskij's predilection for concrete images and employment of the concretizing devices discussed above finds a parallel in his use of a conversational, prosaic tone.   While he shied away from bureaucratic language, he did not indulge in the abstractions so attractive to the Symbolists.   Conversational language, rooted in the everyday world, bespeaks an acceptance of the three-dimensional boundaries of existence corresponding to the world-view of the Acmeists, particularly Mandel'štam's.

Annenskij's use of a conversational tone is related to his reliance upon a persona, who addresses an outside locutor.   (This is a significant element in the verse of Anna Axmatova, and will be discussed below in the Appendix.)   In "Oktjabr'skij mif" ("The October Myth"), he states: "Ja šagi slepogo slyšu." ("I hear the steps of a blind man.").[28]   In "Zaveščanie" ("The Legacy"), he exhorts the novice poet: "A esli pet'- tak pticej poj/ Svobodno, zvonko, smelo."   ("And if you sing, sing like a bird/ Freely, resonantly, boldly.")[29]   One of the most striking instances of conversation occurs in "Za ogradoj" ("Beyond the Fence"), a terrifying lyric in which the moon, grinding a knife in the grass, has been given the power of speech and tells the locutor that he will not escape. ("Mesjac v travax točit nož./ Mesjac vidit, mesjac skažet:/ Ubežiš'. . .da ne ujdeš'. . .").[30]   The tone is not only prosaic, but also has overtones of folk poetry.   The resultant familiarization (for even the educated, sophisticated reader of his time was acquainted with folk tales), like the visual images and the extension of human structures to the natural world, serves to make the images, the lyrics in their entirety concrete, to place them within the confines of the three-dimensional world.

Through personification and the various concretizing devices discussed above, Annenskij has caused his reader to apprehend nature, within the scope of these lyrics, as a sort of human extension.[31] His poetic universe centers on the mind and emotions, is extended to artifacts, includes surrounding nature (particularly the structured nature of the garden), and is limited only by the clouds. Infinity lies beyond the clouds. It occasionally descends to earth in the form of rays of light, or at times manifests itself on the surface as ice crystals. But this is a one-way street; infinity can come to man, but man can never ascend to infinity. Annenskij symbolizes this uni-directional relationship by using images that make the abstract concrete, thereby demonstrating his antipodal differences with Symbolism, which reached upward toward infinity by attempting to make the concrete abstract. His verse constitutes a definitive rejection of Symbolism. With his acceptance of the "three-dimensions of existence" and his emphasis on the intrinsic value of art, he prepared the way for the Acmeist doctrine, most notably for the watershed essay of Mandel'štam.

CHAPTER FOUR

ANNENSKIJ: THE POET AS CRITIC

The advent of Symbolism ushered in a period of experimentation in criticism as well as in poetry and prose. It was at this time that the so-called "aesthetic school" of Russian criticism gained ascendancy over the followers of Vissarion Belinskij, who had been the dominant critics of the mid- to late nineteenth century. Criticism, previously a handmaiden for the advocates of social change, was now accepted as an aspect of the literary craft. As a critic working during this period, Annenskij was a representative of the changed situation. He was a gifted critic whose poetic talents endowed his critical writings with an additional, sensitive dimension.[1] Because his essays are important sources for his opinions regarding contemporary writers and the nature of poetry and the poet, this chapter will analyze his critical works from that point of view. It will furnish the reader with a detailed treatment of those critical views and topics linked with the Acmeist doctrine.

Annenskij's single major critical effort consists of the essays comprising the two collections entitled *kniga otraženij* (*A Book of Reflections*) and *Vtoraja kniga otraženij* (*A Second Book of Reflections*). The first was published in 1906, with the second appearing in 1909.[2] Annenskij proved to be a perceptive critic in these books of essays, although neither drew the attention of the reading public.[3] Both contained pointed, original observations on the writers under consideration. Annenskij's critical approach was psychological and subjective rather than analytical in a formalist sense.[4]

In addition to the books mentioned above, Annenskij published a number of scholarly articles and reviews in such journals as the *Žurnal Ministerstva narodnogo prosveščenija* (*The Journal of the Ministry of Public Education*), *Russkaja škola* (*The Russian School*), and *Filologičeskoe obozrenie* (*The Philological Review*).[5] He also brought out several essays in the journal

Apollon (*Apollo*), including two articles (one of which was divided
into two parts) entitled "O sovremennom lirizme" ("On
Contemporary Lyricism"), in which he discussed his contemporaries
in detail.[6] Their reaction against this work was, understandably,
heated, for Annenskij broke with tradition by treating established
and beginning poets with equal respect.[7] He embellished his essays
with digressive comments on the personalities of his subjects, with
observations on poetics, and with bits of historical data.[8]
Annenskij's sensitive analysis and clever comments and jokes
enhance "On Contemporary Lyricism," but his style is uneven,
with the analyses of the individual poets sketchy, almost in outline
form.[9] His divergence from Symbolism, in keeping with his
eclecticism and independence, is evident from his rather cavalier
attitude toward established poets, his practice of shifting from topic
to topic, and his witty asides to the reader.[10]

Annenskij published two articles that are pedagogical as well
as critical: "Stixotvorenija Ja. P. Polonskogo kak pedagogičeskij
material" ("The Verse of Ja. P. Polonskij as Pedagogical Material")
and "Sočinenija gr. A. K. Tolstogo kak pedagogičeskij material"
("The Works of Count A. K. Tolstoj as Pedagogical Material").
Both of these essays, appearing in the journal *Vospitanie i obučenie*
(*Education and Instruction*) provide insights into Annenskij's
aesthetic views.[11] They will be discussed below.

Annenskij devoted a number of critical essays to
nineteenth-century Russian writers. Two of them dealing with
Nikolaj Gogol', "Problema Gogolevskogo jumora" ("The Problem of
Gogolian Humor") and "Èstetika *Mertvyx duš* i ee nasled'e" ("The
Aesthetics of *Dead Souls* and its Legacy"), appeared in *Kniga
otraženij* and *Apollon*, respectively.[12] His examinations of Fedor
Dostoevskij and Anton Čexov were published in *Kniga otrazenij*, as
was an essay on Turgenev,[13] and one on Mixail Lermontov, "Ob
èstetičeskom otnošenii Lermontova k prirode" ("On Lermontov's
Aesthetic Attitude toward Nature") came out in *Russkaja škola*
(*The Russian School*).

Annenskij's critical writings about contemporary literature
centered on Russian Symbolism and several of the future Acmeists.
In spite of his interest in French poetry, attested to by his
translations of the French Parnassians and Symbolists and by the
closeness of his aesthetic views to those of the French, he devoted
only one scholarly article to French poets.[14] But he was less
reticent about the Russians, and both "On Contemporary Lyricism"

and "Bal'mont lirik" ("Bal'mont the Lyricist") dealt with Russian Symbolism.[15]   In the first, he named four Symbolist poets, Konstantin Bal'mont, Valerij Brjusov, Vjačeslav Ivanov, and Fedor Sologub, who seemed to him to typify modern Russian poetry. Although he asserted that contemporary verse rarely expressed the "sincerity and charm" exemplified by the poetry of Puškin's school, Annenskij considered it more "exact."   He maintained that it possessed greater variety than did Russian "classical" poetry and was better able to convey a particular mood.[16]   But Annenskij's detachment from Symbolism is evident at the beginning of the essay, for he declared here that the oddities of the Symbolist style were no longer striking, adding that Symbolism had lost its revolutionary novelty and had acquired the rigidity of an accepted movement.[17]   He considered the term "Symbolist," moreover, to be inaccurate, arguing that the ballads of Valerij Brjusov could not definitely be regarded as Symbolist.[18]

   Annenskij's criticism of the Russian Symbolist movement extended from a disparagement of Symbolism in general to criticism of Bal'mont in particular, and to other Symbolist writers as well.   He offered caustic observations on the poetry of Belyj, Blok, and Brjusov.   Annenskij declared that Belyj simply did not know which of his muses was smiling at him at any one time, implying that the noted poet vacillated according to his passing mood or inclination.[19]   Regarding Blok (correctly) as an "innate Symbolist," Annenskij maintained that " . . . Blok's perceptions are shifting, [his] words are elastic, and his verses . . . cannot but be Symbolist."[20]   Annenskij's treatment of Brjusov was more extensive and negative; he asserted that Brjusov loved the "beautiful phantom of life, dream, adorned with metaphors, more than life itself."   He felt that Brjusov's poetry was a "chronicle of uninterrupted apprenticeship and self-verification."   For Brjusov, everything had become only "shadows," simply "stages of future creative work."   Even the erotic elements were, he felt, not so much an expression of sexual love as they were the "process of creation, that is, the sacred play with words . . . ."   For Brjusov, he maintained, love was associated with heroics, with the image of the poet.   But he praised Brjusov as well, declaring that no one was more gifted at showing the disgusting futility of life lurking behind the cold beauty of poetry.[21]

   Annenskij's relationship with the Acmeist poet Nikolaj Gumilev extended to two critical works, "On Contemporary

Lyricism," part two, and an article recently brought to light by
Gleb Struve. In "On Contemporary Lyricism," Annenskij wrote
that Gumilev was more a poet of colors than outlines and was
more "elegant than musically beautiful." His statement suggests
that Gumilev's visual images were more indefinite, less obviously
linear, than those of Annenskij himself. Annenskij praised the
younger poet for having expended a great deal of effort in the
composition of his poetry, verse in which he sometimes attained an
almost Gallic precision.[22] In any event, Annenskij regarded
Gumilev's work as marking a definitive change from the musical,
often vague and abstract images of later Symbolist verse.

In his preface to Annenskij's above-mentioned essay on
Gumilev, Struve states that Annenskij followed the aesthetic
development of the younger poet with interest. Struve further
holds that Annenskij knew a significant portion of Gumilev's verse
that had been published up to that time, especially the collection
Žemčuga (The Pearl).[23] Annenskij admired the original beauty of
Gumilev's style, noting the younger poet's ability to observe
astutely and to describe what he had seen. He complimented
Gumilev on an ability to define a theme clearly and develop it
well.[24]

Annenskij's aesthetic views are scattered throughout the body
of his critical writings, appearing, for instance, in his essays on
Greek tragedy as well as in those about Mixail Lermontov or
Bal'mont. He clearly intended that his criticism function
principally as a vehicle to convey his thoughts about art, with the
individual writer under consideration relegated to secondary
importance. Maintaining that art was independent of any outside
purpose, Annenskij asserted that poetry was primarily an
intellectual process and that creativity and torment were related.
In his study of Lermontov, "On the Aesthetic Relation of
Lermontov to Nature," Annenskij stated that poetry was "art first
of all." "In that," he continued, lay its "charm, the unfading
nature of its glory, and its tragedy." Poets, he added, were a
breed apart. Annenskij believed that poetry "did not serve anyone
or anything," that it was "free." The creative work of the artist
was amoral, he declared, for the autonomy of aesthetics placed art
outside of morality.[25] In spite of his not having broken with
Russian nineteenth-century civic poets, Annenskij did not follow
their dictum that art had a special social obligation.

In "Tragičeskaja Medeja" ("Tragic Medea"), a work

demonstrating his interest in the culture of ancient Greece, Annenskij regretted the neglect of poetry as a rational process. Poetry, he said, should never forfeit its intellectual nuances. In order to take pleasure in the "divine ravings" of the poet, the reader had to master his "sharp and excited thought."[26] He regarded poetic composition as the offshoot of conscious stylistic analysis, a view related to his visual, linear approach to art.[27] Annenskij differed, therefore, from the later Symbolists, for whom poetry was a medium of mystical escape from the mundane, in his insistence upon the intellectual foundation of poetry. In his metapoetry, too, Annenskij regarded poetic inspiration as the source of creativity, affirming at the same time that the creative process is a rational one. While the younger Symbolists adhered to Vladimir Solov'ev's doctrine that wisdom or beauty was a transcendent being with whom the seeker could unite mystically, Annenskij disagreed, suggesting that beauty, although external, was not transcendent. It could be defined and expressed through poetry.[28]

Annenskij felt that beauty and suffering were simultaneously linked, yet opposed. "The negative, morbid strength of torment," he stated, is "counterbalanced in poetry by the strength of beauty, in which the possibility of happiness is contained."[29] In essence, he wrote, poetry is "the most vivid denial of suffering . . . ." In no place is the "tragic role of poetry displayed with such intensity as in depictions of torment."[30] For its creator, poetry becomes the means of escaping from suffering. It is only in the contemplation of beauty (the essence of poetry, of all art) that the poet may attain some degree of happiness. Through the creative act, he can provisionally forget suffering. Annenskij's conception of art as tragedy suggests that the purpose of art (beautiful form) is to counteract the suffering depicted in it. Perhaps the poet's suffering, expressed also in such lyrics as "The Bow and Strings," "The Barrel Organ," and "After the Concert," is a manifestation of his awareness that beauty does not always provide relief from man's transitory state, especially when that beauty is expressed through the "temporary" medium of sound rather than the "permanence" of the visual image. Annenskij's insistence on formal structure as the primary component of art skirts the thematic emphasis of the civic poets and critics and links him with Puškin. Similarly, Annenskij's supposition that the beauty of (visual) art offers an alternative to the suffering of existence within the confines of time is an echo of ideas developed in his verse. He maintained that the work existed apart from its creator (which can be seen especially in "The Bronze Poet"), and did not, he asserted, die with the artist.[31]

In those critical writings on poetic technique, Annenskij stressed the enormous significance of language and the importance of the word as a means of poetic expression. He left a sizable body of essays about language, including reviews of Russian grammars and language textbooks and an article on the language and poetry of the Russian North.[32] Poetry, said Annenskij, has to be expressed by means of words, themselves symbols of psychic acts. The pictorial distinctness of poetry is derived from its use of the word.[33] He has once again made the connection, this time in his poetry, between the word and the visual image and linearity (distinctness). In his pedagogical writings, Annenskij stressed the importance of the spoken language for mastery of the written word, stating that the oral and written word are intimately connected.[34] He has not shifted his orientation here from the visual to the aural image, but rather has emphasized the need for, the significance of, prosaisms or everyday language in poetry. Once more, he has underscored the link between the visual, the concrete, the common, and art. Poetry, he wrote, is the highest manifestation of the creative power of speech. He maintained that it was impossible to know a language without having studied its poetry, asserting that the converse of this was also true.[35] It is because of this emphasis on "actual" language that he roundly condemned the "dulling" of the language inevitably resulting from the infiltration of bookish, official–urban usage.[36]

Annenskij's emphasis on the word as the "aesthetically valuable manifestation from the sphere of the most ancient and most subtle of arts"[37] is paralleled by his linkage of poetry and the clarity of ideas. He felt that the art of the word, poetry, was the medium through which the "integral, clear, perfect, and rational world of ideas" could be transmitted.[38] His stress on rationality, on ideas, as the basis of poetry and his concomitant accentuation of the word as the medium through which they are expressed are related to his supposition that beautiful form is the essence of art. The special importance he gives to the word is linked to the Acmeists' emphasis on the word as a building block in the structure of poetry, a concept particularly important to Mandel'štam.

In "The Verse of Ja. P. Polonskij as Pedagogical Material," Annenskij mentioned three major devices of poetry: comparison, analysis, and synthesis. Comparison is expressed through the metaphor, parallelism, and allegory. It acquires "nuances of negation, hyperbole, irony, and various forms of contrast." Annenskij's use of comparison, discussed in the third chapter, is one of his favored means of rendering the abstract image concrete. Analysis, he felt, endows an object or phenomenon with those characteristics usually associated with a given object, yet another way of comparing, ultimately, of "concretizing." He considered the epithet a prime example of such analysis; actually it could be regarded as a means of concentrating a poetic image, of making it concrete. The function of analysis was "to unite the separate poetic strokes" into an artistic whole.[39] Once again, the emphasis is on linearity, on separate "rays" converging to form a planar structure. The similarity between this conception and visual experiments taking place in the plastic arts only a few years later is both striking and significant.

Annenskij separates the poet from the reader in his critical writings as well as in his verse, for poetic creativity is linked with suffering that the artist alone endures. The "providential purpose of the poet," he declared, "lies in the enduring of a complex inner life, in the agitated and passionate search for beauty." Because of the "disharmony" of this search with the "prose of life," the poet suffers, but art is born from his suffering.[40] Annenskij numbered the poet among the elect in his essay on Bal'mont, stating that it is "worth living and suffering in order to hear what others do not hear."[41] The view he expressed here is related to that found in "After the Concert" - that the artist alone is privileged to perceive beauty. The "prose of life" is an allusion to the non-artistic majority, whose disparate actions mesh together to form a prosaic counterpart to those of the poet. Because of his driving search for beauty, which the non-artist cannot really comprehend, the poet differs from the majority of his fellows.

Annenskij set the poet apart from society, but he did not absolve him from labor. The poet was to be a craftsman. In "The Aesthetic Relation of Lermontov to Nature," Annenskij stated: "We give him [the poet] coal, and he gives us back a diamond." Creativity was the result of hard work.[42] The poet who transforms coal is not merely a worker, for the conversion of coal into the diamond involves an enormous effort and pressure equated

with the poet's suffering. It is the quintessential change that
defines art, that change from ugliness, from the utilitarian, into
beauty. His assertion admits of two possible interpretations. First,
the poet is a craftsman creating art through conscious effort. This
is a pointed rejoinder to the earlier Symbolists' conception that the
poet occupied an elevated position, as well as to the mysticism
central to the aesthetic vision of the later poets. The medium in
which the poet creates is the crucible of his own torment. The
poet's suffering is the subject of several lyrics, including "After the
Concert," "The Bow and Strings," and "The Barrel Organ."
Suffering not only underscores the poet's mortality, but also stresses
that the poet does not transcend the world of reality, the
three-dimensional, temporal world, but rather creates within its
confines.

Annenskij's literary criticism covers a wide range both
temporally and culturally, from the tragedians of the classical
Greek theater to his own contemporaries. His aesthetic views run
like a thread through all of these essays. *The Book of Reflections*
and *The Second Book of Reflections* are aptly named for, in a
sense, all of the writers with whom Annenskij dealt were only
reflectors for his ideas, media for his views on art and its relation
to the artist, particularly the poet.

Annenskij's aesthetic values might seem at first glance to be
contradictory. On one hand, he declares that art is not dependent
on external considerations, that the basis of poetry is language,
specifically the word, and that the poet is a craftsman who, by his
own effort, produces beautiful art. On the other, he suggests that
beauty is closely linked to a higher good, implying further that the
poet can create beauty (art) only because he has been chosen to
suffer frustration in his attempts to express perfect beauty. These
apparent contradictions can be resolved, however, when we recall
the thematic analysis of the second chapter. The encompassing
power of time includes everything but art (symbolized by the
statue of Puškin in "The Bronze Poet"). Art means poetry to
Annenskij, but this poetry is emblemized by the visual image, not
by sound. The word as the basic building block of verse
corresponds to the visual, physical, concrete world. While the poet
is a craftsman working with materials (words), the beauty he
perceives and transforms into verse (the poetry of the lyric
"Poetry," the light in "Into the Magic Prism") transcends the

actuality.   More to the point, it conquers time, symbol of the
banality, the anguish ("toska") of physical existence that ties man
down and limits him (the gravestone in "Lilacs on the Stone,"
anguish in "The Steel Cicada").   The suffering of the poet stems
from two causes.   First, the artist lives in his own world, creates
alone (the singer in "After the Concert," the poet alone in the
Sinai in "Poetry"); he is separate from society, subject to the
loneliness and anxiety of his situation.   Second, he himself cannot
escape time, a certainty of the shortness of life, a constant
awareness of its banality.   The beauty he perceives (the white light
from "Into the Magic Prism," the footprints of poetry in "Poetry")
is not the beauty he creates, for his consciousness alters his vision
into actuality existing on a lower level.   But it is beauty
nevertheless and, as such, succeeds in eluding the powerful grip of
time.   If the poet suffers because he himself is prisoner of the
physical world, he nevertheless transforms beauty, through art, into
a component of that world.   As an inspired craftsman, he triumphs
over it.

The seeming ambiguity of Annenskij's views is a mark of his
unique position within contemporary Russian literature.   He joined
no school, subscribed to no accepted philosophy, and, in short,
went his own way.   He differs from the Symbolists in the emphasis
he places on form, specifically the word, in his preference for the
visual over the aural image, in his view that the poet was a
craftsman.   Even Brjusov, who resembled him in a stress upon the
necessity for clarity in verse, diverged from Annenskij in his
emphasis on the artist at the expense of art.   It was Annenskij
alone, in his criticism as well as his verse, who posited the poet as
a craftsman working with concrete, actual materials in the temporal
world, a figure who would be the immediate ancestor of the
Acmeists.

CHAPTER FIVE

THE ACMEISTS AND THEIR DOCTRINE

"In the winter of 1912-1913," stated the Formalist critic Viktor Žirmunskij, "several young poets consciously separated themselves from Symbolism as a literary school. . . They called their new trend. . .'Acmeism'. . . ."[1] Acmeism shouldered its way forward approximately three years after the crisis in Symbolism, a crisis marked by the split between Brjusov and "clarism" on one hand and Vjačeslav Ivanov, Andrej Belyj, and "mysticism" on the other. The Acmeists included in their number such new poets as Anna Axmatova, Osip Mandel'štam, Nikolaj Gumilev, and Sergej Gorodeckij, the latter two having published the essays in 1913 that marked the formal birth of the new school.[2] The new poets were neither as "unsociable" as the Symbolists nor as "loud" as the Futurists but, "having cast aside all shyness, they strove to succeed."[3]

The Acmeists were closely related to but not synonymous with the organization immediately preceding them known as the "Cex poètov" ("The Guild of Poets"), and many of the Acmeists, including Gumilev, Gorodeckij, Axmatova, Mandel'štam, Vladimir Narbut, Georgij Adamovič, and Georgij Ivanov, were in the Guild too. The Guild, its beginnings predating the start of Acmeism, was in existence between 1911 and 1914, and both the Guild and Acmeism were founded under the stimulus of Gumilev.[4]

In addition to their tie with the Guild of Poets, the Acmeists were also linked to the "Obščestvo revnitelej xudožestvennogo slova" ("Society of the Partisans of the Artistic Word"). This group numbered Acmeists as well as Symbolists among its members, and Vjačeslav Ivanov belonged to it, as did Aleksandr Blok. Members of the "Society" participated in discussions and readings of original literary works.[5]

Nikolaj Gumilev, founder of Acmeism, was born in 1886 and shot as a counter-revolutionary in late August, 1921.[6] The eight collections of his lyrics went through two editions within his lifetime.[7] His career as a critic was launched with the appearance of an essay in the Paris review *Sirius* in 1907; starting in November, 1909, he began to write for *Apollon* (*Apollo*), and it was in this journal that his contribution to the Acmeist doctrine, "Zavety simvolizma i akmeizm" ("The Precepts of Symbolism, and Acmeism") first appeared. Gumilev's "Pis'ma o russkoj poèzii" ("Letters on Russian Poetry"), scattered through *Apollon* between 1909 and 1916, were collected and published separately in 1923.[8]

Sergej Gorodeckij (1884-1967) produced twenty-eight volumes of poetry.[9] His critical essays appeared in *Apollon* beside those of Gumilev and, like the latter, Gorodeckij wrote his own "Pis'ma of russkoj poèzii" ("Letters on Russian Poetry"), which came out in *Apollon* over a period of time. Gorodeckij was not nearly as significant a critic as Gumilev and was much less gifted as a poet. He was, moreover, an opportunist, oriented toward any literary movement that happened to be gaining the ascendancy.[10]

Osip Mandel'štam was a member of "Cex poètov" and an Acmeist from the inception of the movement.[11] Born in Warsaw in January, 1891, Mandel'štam was arrested on the 2nd of May, 1938, and probably died sometime during that year.[12] His first verse was published in the July-August, 1910 issue of *Apollon*, and his first collection of poems, *Kamen'* (*Stone*), came out in 1913.[13] In addition to his poetry, Mandel'štam also wrote prose fiction and a good many critical articles, showing himself in the process to be a sensitive, incisive critic.[14] "Utro akmeizma" ("The Morning of Acmeism") was probably written in 1912, followed by "O sobesednike" ("About the Interlocutor") in 1913, "Slovo i kul'tura" ("The Word and Culture") in 1921, and "O prirode slova" ("On the Nature of the Word") and "Burja i natisk" ("Sturm und Drang") in 1922 and 1923, respectively.[15]

It was Anna Axmatova [Gorenko] (1881-1965), who, perhaps more than any of the other poets of the school, used conversational language and everyday detail in her verse.[16] She made her debut in the early 1900's and was immensely popular.[17] Axmatova was a lyrical poet whose early work featured a persona with an intriguing, intricate private life, a world of complicated relationships expressed in simple, direct language.

While the two Symbolist groups were influenced, respectively, by the French Symbolists and German and Russian philosophers, the Acmeists instead looked to the French Parnassians. Like them,

the Acmeists emphasized the importance of form, striving to create
a pictorial quality in their art, in contrast to the sound orientation
of Symbolism.[18]   Although Gumilev objected to the Parnassian
tendency to treat the word as mere object, the Parnassians as well
as the Acmeists stressed the significance of the word.[19]   The
Acmeists subscribed to the Parnassian belief in art for art's sake,
and Gumilev was especially close to them in his view that art is a
state of equilibrium which is "solid, firm, and durable."[20]

Besides José Maria de Hérédia, the two Parnassians most
important for the Acmeists were Leconte de Lisle and Théophile
Gautier.[21]   Like Hérédia, Leconte de Lisle was interested in the
exotic, drawn to the "splendid savagery of primitive cultures and
past epochs."[22]   Gumilev touched on Gautier in his essay "The
Precepts of Symbolism, and Acmeism," regarding the Parnassian as
a poetic model not only for his emphasis on poetic form and his
theory of art for art's sake, but also for his pictorial sensuousness.[23]
A veritable cult of Gautier developed among the Acmeists.[24]

The Acmeists would appear to have advocated evolutionary,
not revolutionary change from Symbolism, causing some critics to
assert that the newer school did not represent any significant
change.   Victor Erlich, who referred to Acmeism as an outgrowth
of Symbolism, a "Symbolist heresy," maintained that Gumilev
remained "within the limits of the same poetic pattern and the
same social pattern."[25]   He is not alone.   Other critics have also
held that Acmeism, a continuation of Symbolism, did not represent
anything new.   "The Acmeists," says William Chalsma, "wrote in
the reformed Symbolist modes."[26]   To others, Acmeism was not
even a continuation of Symbolism but represented rather a step
back from it.[27]   Clarence Brown has remarked that, "for a
modernist movement in verse, Acmeism was curiously conservative
both in theme and technique."   Brown thought that the rhymes
and meters of Mandel'štam might "seem familiar to the
contemporaries of Puškin."[28]   The Acmeists, Boris Èjxenbaum
charged, did not change tradition, but rather preserved it.[29]

The apparent conservatism of Acmeism surely derives more
from their acknowledged function as a crucial segment in the larger
cultural continuum than from any intrinsic opposition to change,
and certain critics have felt that Acmeism actually represents a
dramatic shift from Symbolism; Viktor Žirmunskij based his famous
essay, "Preodolevšie simvolizm" ("Those Who have Overcome
Symbolism"), on that very supposition.[30]   For B. Sajanov, the

Acmeists differed from the Symbolists not only in their aesthetics, but in the philosophical basis for aesthetic perception as well. It was a difference between a system based on the perceived world, specifically the visual world of the everyday, and the world of suggestion. "Between the world view of the Acmeists and the world view of the majority of the Symbolists," he asserted, lay "an entire epoch."[31]   Gleb Struve remarked that Acmeism was successful in its struggle against Symbolism, even though in his view it may have failed as a literary theory; Acmeism, he stated, succeeded insofar as it was the reaction of a group of poets against some aspects of Symbolism. It was Acmeism, not Symbolism, whose descendants were active after the Revolution.[32]   Less innovative than Futurism in poetic technique, Acmeism, in its emphasis on the intrinsic value of art and on literary form as the focal point of the creative effort, nevertheless represented a dramatic change from Symbolism.[33]

The Acmeists countered Symbolist indefiniteness with verse that was "graphic, clear, and reasonable," opposing clarity to the indistinct poetry of the Symbolists. Like their mentor Annenskij, the Acmeists made use of "concretism," a direct reference to an object existing in a concrete world, in contrast to the allusions and hints of the Symbolists.[34]

The clarity of style that was central to Acmeism necessitated a complementary emphasis on the intrinsic value of the word as a means of artistic expression. For the Symbolists, the word was important for its musical suggestiveness, but the Acmeists believed that it had a self-contained value.[35] "The Acmeists," said Erlich, "tended to reduce the gap between the poetic idiom and cognitive speech," and they discarded the "esoteric allusiveness and studied ambiguity" of Symbolism.[36] And the Acmeists also rejected the Symbolist tenet that words were related to each other by secret correspondences. Gumilev asserted that this belief reflected the influence of German mysticism on Symbolism, and both he and Gorodeckij opposed this facet of Symbolist aesthetics with their conception of the innate value of words.[37] Their use of conversational linguistic elements exemplified the Acmeists' view of language as a concrete, intrinsically significant entity.[38] The Acmeists' insistence on clarity and definiteness was related to their use of visual images, in contrast to the Symbolists' preoccupation with sound.[39] The former rejected the musical orientation of Symbolism in favor of poetry which, in its employment of lines and colors, could more readily be compared with the plastic arts.[40] The verse of Mandel'štam contained structural, specifically architectural elements comparable to those found in Annenskij's poetry. The Acmeists favored the depiction of the objects of the external world in clear outlines; they loved intense color, the sharp outlines of forms, detail, and the symmetry and restrained measurement of lines.[41]   All of these visual, indeed spatial details were contained in Annenskij's aesthetic world.   One facet of the Acmeists' inclination toward clarity, definiteness, and pictorial distinctness was their emphasis on logic in art, in contradistinction to the later Symbolists' view of art as a system of mystical transcendence in which logic would have little place.[42]

The differences between the Acmeists and Symbolists extend beyond their attitudes about poetic form to include their views of poetry and the poet.   For the second generation of Symbolists, the poet was essentially a priest for whom poetry was a prayer, perhaps, in the case of Blok, to Sophia.   The Symbolist poets as a group were not concerned with an auditor, but favored a cult of the individual poet not necessarily interested in communication at all.

The Acmeists countered this conception of the poet as seer with their belief that poetry was craftsmanship, a workshop, an idea embodied in the program, indeed the very name, of the related Guild of Poets group.   The poet's "spiritual knowledge," a view peculiar to Symbolism, was replaced by the hypothesis that the poet's knowledge is limited, but, at the same time, the Acmeists believed that art is a "sacred craft."[43]   The emphasis here is on the word "craft," for the Acmeists regarded art as possessing intrinsic worth as beautiful form, opposing the Symbolist vision that art necessarily serves a higher purpose.

The aesthetic gap between Acmeism and Symbolism was reflected also in their world views.   Life for the Symbolists was tragic, and the poet's relationship to life was expressed in his anguish, despair, and presentiment of annihilation.[44]   The dominant moods of Symbolist poetry were emptiness, resignation, boredom, and indifference to surroundings.   Traces of this atmosphere can be detected in Annenskij's verse dating from this period; his pessimism is superficially akin to the predominant mood of Symbolist verse, yet Annenskij's dim atmosphere results rather from his acceptance of the limitations of existence than from an attempt to surmount them in the fashion of his contemporaries.   The Acmeists substituted joy in life, optimism, and delight in their craft for the Symbolists' pessimism, creating poetry in a "major" key.[45]

The Symbolist view of the poet as a seer, with poetry primarily significant as a means to a higher end, is linked to their belief that poetry is rather a mystical experience than a form of art.[46] They sought higher, "eternal" values through art. The Acmeists opposed the "predominance of the spiritual over the concrete" and were immersed in reality, in a physical and intellectual reality reflected particularly in the poetic themes of Mandel'štam.[47] "If the Ego-Futurists," declared the critic L'vov-Rogačevskij, "were creators of *words*, then the Adamists were the creators of *things*."[48] The examination of the Acmeist doctrine below demonstrates that they did not create "things" at the expense of words. The Acmeists' framework of artistic values can be seen readily in the set of essays called, for purposes of this discussion, the Acmeist doctrine. It was the sudden appearance of Gumilev's and Gorodeckij's articles that in fact signaled the beginnings of the Acmeist movement, for Mandel'štam's contibution was not published until 1919.[49] Acmeist aesthetics as expressed in the essays consisted of certain major points. Art should deal with the real world, which necessitates a rejection of the unclear images peculiar to the Symbolists, repudiating also the Symbolist view that art should depict the unknowable. Each manifestation of life should have intrinsic aesthetic value, The Acmeists opposed clarity and distinctness of images to the Symbolists' theory of correspondences and use of suggestion as the foundation of their verse.[50] The Acmeists' stress upon clarity was reflected in an emphasis on the individual word and on the significance of art.[51]

Any detailed analysis of Acmeism must necessarily take into account Mixail Kuzmin's essay "O prekrasnoj jasnosti" ("On Beautiful Clarity"), in which he preceded the Acmeists in establishing some of the principles they themselves were later to espouse.[52] Kuzmin asserted that clarity had to be reintroduced into literature, specifically into prose, that the writer should "write logically, observing the purity of popular speech." The writer should always bear in mind the correspondence between a particular form and a given style of writing and must be as skillful as an architect in the details as he would be in the work as a whole. His style ought to be clear and comprehensible, for lyricism belongs in poetry, and he should "love the word as Flaubert did."[53]

Kuzmin's connection with Acmeism, originally considered quite close, has recently been regarded as more tenuous. Sam Driver questioned the existence of a tie between them, citing Axmatova's view that the identification of Kuzmin as herald to the new movement was due to a mistake made initially by Boris Žirmunskij in 1916 and repeated dutifully by critics ever since.[54] But Kuzmin was definitely not a Symbolist within the parameters of this work, and at best could be regarded as a transitional figure between the two schools.[55] He deliberately ignored the Symbolists in his essay and designated himself as "writer-authority" in matters of aesthetic theory, a model for younger writers. (His essay, published in *Apollon*, was almost certainly directed at the Acmeists.) His attitude is underscored by his use of command forms of verbs throughout. Given the fact, moreover, that poetry was the dominant literary form during this period, Kuzmin's attention to young prose writers at the expense of the poets might seem surprising at first glance, as might his suggestion that French prosaists serve as examples for Russian novices. His implication may well have been that, in view of the mystical haziness and lack of distinctness with which poetry had come to be associated,[56] clarity could be attained only in the composition of prose. Rather than a directive to discourage young poets, his essay should rather be considered a criticism of current poetic practice, a sarcastic broadside aimed at the excesses of later Symbolism. With poetry discredited by the Symbolists, he hints, the only decent remaining literature is prose. But Kuzmin was not really anti-poetic, only anti-Symbolist, and his essay, in spite of Axmatova's disclaimer, eased the way for the Acmeist doctrine.

Why was it not possible for the Acmeists (or Futurists) to write without resorting to public manifestoes? To answer this question, we must return to the supposition given in Chapter One, that the principal driving forces of modernism were its constant search for change and its attempt to posit new parameters for placing the arts within the context of what must surely have been regarded as an increasingly complex and incomprehensible society. Because Russian literature, beginning in the eighteenth century, came to be a vehicle for philosophical conjecturing and social criticism as well as art, it was natural for belles-lettres to assume extra-literary duties during the modernist revolt. The manifestoes of modernism took the place of the previously established boundaries of a world now frighteningly out of control, and art was thrust forward as a new system, a new "ectoblast." Each of the modernist groups dealt with this change in its own way, each positing art as a philosophical construct (in the case of Symbolism, a religion) with its accompanying set of "dogma," the manifesto or doctrine.

Both Gumilev and Gorodeckij read their essays aloud at the Petersburg literary cabaret "Brodjačaja sobaka" ("The Stray Dog") on December 19, 1912, prior to publication in *Apollon*.[57] Both the Acmeists and the Futurists indulged in this "political campaigning" for their new schools, and this conscious, concerted effort to sway public taste (even by offending it in the case of Futurism) must be considered a component of modernism, not only in Russia, but in the West as well.

Gumilev introduced his essay, "The Precepts of Symbolism, and Acmeism," with the assertion that Symbolism was no longer a developing school of poetry. ". . .Symbolism," he stated, ". . . .is now in decline. . .[with]. . .Symbolist works . . .hardly appearing at all. . . ." Gumilev posited that Acmeism (from the Greek "acme," the highest level of something) or Adamism (from the founding human Adam, implying a manly, firm, and clear view of life) had arisen in place of Symbolism. It is significant that one of Gumilev's reasons for pushing Acmeism is the excuse that very few Symbolist works were currently being published; obviously he was distressed over a cultural vacuum, considering it a dangerous absence of structure, and felt that Acmeism was vital as a replacement school. But Gumilev did not completely repudiate Symbolism or the significance of the Symbolists, maintaining that "Symbolism was a worthy father" to Acmeism.[58] He went on nevertheless to criticize and, finally, to reject Symbolism as a poetic school, considering it no longer viable as a modern movement, and the remainder of his essay consists of a point-by-point comparison between Symbolism and Acmeism, with the latter emerging in each instance, not surprisingly, as the preferable alternative.

Gumilev contrasted the Romanic and Germanic "spirits," identifying Acmeism with the Romanic, the Mediterranean world. French Symbolism, he insisted, had concentrated on purely literary problems, questions of stylistics such as free verse, a more original and malleable style, and the elevation of the metaphor "above everything else," as well as on the "notorious theory of correspondences." He asserted that French Symbolism had rejected, so far as aesthetics were concerned, the Romanic spirit.

This was a spirit drawn to light and expressing itself in clarity and a distinctness between objects. Gumilev felt that the vagueness and murkiness of French Symbolism were closer, in fact, to the Germanic spirit than to the Romanic one. According to Gumilev, it was the Acmeists who were the heirs of the Romanic spirit, a spirit temporarily eclipsed by the suggestions and amorphousness of Symbolism. The contemporary reader would have had to assume that, although Russian Symbolism was literally heir to the French, it had actually drawn its inspiration from a German model.[59]

Gumilev felt that the Acmeists could counter the intricacies of the metaphor as developed by the Symbolists with "living, national speech," advocating a shift in style from complexity and incomprehensibility to simplicity. In addition, he thought that a certain degree of Romanic irreverence or irony was a positive change from the Germanic seriousness characterizing Symbolism. Although Gumilev respected the Symbolists for having demonstrated the significance of the symbol in poetry, he did not believe that all other means of poetic expression should be sacrificed to it.[60]

Gumilev opposed the "revolt" of the "Germanic" Symbolists against the environment of independent phenomena, charging that the Acmeist recognized his position within nature as a phenomenon among other phenomena. ". . .We become involved in a world rhythm."[61] His incorporation of man within nature was linked with a related condemnation of the mysticism peculiar to later Symbolism, which had, he felt, overstepped its limits in its fascination with "mysticism, with theosophy, with occultism." For this he substituted the Acmeist tenet that the unknowable must be accepted as being beyond human comprehension. It was presumptuous of art to feel that it could provide a means for understanding the unknowable and, furthermore, the realization of this impossibility could be pleasing.[62]

Gumilev concluded his essay with a brief discussion of the four writers he considered most significant for Acmeism: Shakespeare, Rabelais, Villon, and Théophile Gautier. Each of them, he stated, was a "cornerstone for the building of Acmeism," and his terminology as well as his choices stresses the architect–craftsman image of the Acmeist poet. Shakespeare had revealed the inner world of man, Rabelais had shown the joys of the body, Villon had told the Acmeists about life, and Théophile Gautier had "found in art the worthy garb of irreproachable forms for this life."[63]   These four writers can be construed as corresponding to the four humors or the four directions, definitive cornerstones incorporating four different components of art.

The primary significance of Gumilev's essay lies in its condemnation of Symbolism and concomitant presentation of the basic tenets of Acmeism.   Curiously, he lambasts Symbolism primarily as a philosophical system and only secondarily as a literary school, his basic criticism being that Symbolism, having borrowed heavily from the "Germanic" [philosophical] spirit, was hopelessly entangled in mystical cogitations.   This emphasis is compatible with the larger role literature had taken on during this period, a purpose at once metaphysical and aesthetic, that was central to the discussion of Chapter One of the present study. The main purpose of literature, as viewed by contemporary writers, was to provide a framework for a confusing barrage of stimulae. The attainment of this goal was preliminary to and linked with aesthetic concerns, and that is why it was so important for Gumilev to counter Symbolist mysticism before positing Acmeist clarity as a viable substitute.   Acmeism, he declared, could correct the philosophical excesses of Symbolism by clearly delineating the knowable world, i.e., whatever man could definitely perceive and express in art with a certain degree of authority, from the unknowable world lying beyond one's cognizance.   Gumilev found the Symbolist "leap of faith" both incomprehensible and reprehensible.

Apart from asserting that Acmeism would make use of "living national speech" and reject the complexities and metaphors of the Symbolists and their Germanic seriousness in favor of simplicity and Romanic irreverence, Gumilev touched on poetic style only in passing.   He did not give detailed directions to the Acmeists.   This may have been a deliberate oversight designed to allow the Acmeists maximum freedom in poetic style, although he probably felt that he could draw more young poets into the movement by restraining his natural tendency to dominate.   His attitude contrasts with that of Kuzmin, who outlined those stylistic methods that would later define Acmeism with far greater precision and clarity than did Gumilev himself.   Gumilev's principal concern would seem to have been that of positing Acmeism as a poetic school divorced from Symbolism, and justifying this separation on aesthetic grounds only after having first destroyed the philosophical underpinnings of his rival.   He may well have neglected, however, to outline a more specific program.

      Gorodeckij's "Nekotorye tečenija v sovremennoj russkoj poèzii" ("Some Tendencies in Contemporary Russian Poetry") had less of an impact than Gumilev's essay, for Gorodeckij attempted primarily to elaborate on some of Gumilev's assertions in an effort to adapt Acmeist theory to the previously existing poetic publications of Cex poètov.[64]   The introduction to "Several Tendencies" was constructed along the same lines as Gumilev's, for Gorodeckij stated that "the Symbolist movement in Russia. . . [was]. . .finished."   He felt that Symbolism, riddled with internal flaws, contained the seeds of its own destruction.   Gorodeckij held that art was a state of equilibrium and solidity, but that Symbolism had disregarded these laws in an attempt to "make use of the fluidity of the word. . . ."   The theories of Potebnja having established the mobility of thought behind the word or combinations of words, the Symbolists, he charged, had made use of this mobility and had therefore "destroyed the. . . prerogative of art—to be tranquil in all of its propositions and. . .methods."

      The Symbolists, he continued, felt that comprehensible poetry was banal, and they mistakenly brought in elements extraneous to it (such as the mysticism of Vjačeslav Ivanov).   Gorodeckij asserted that Symbolism was not the "spokesman of the spirit of Russia. . . Symbolism was the method of our Symbolists."[65]   It was clear that Gorodeckij intended rather for the Acmeists to be that spokesman, setting up the parameters that would define and direct historical development as well as aesthetics.   He concluded that Symbolism, "having filled the world with 'correspondences,' had turned it into a forfeit. . . ."   The actual, physical world was important to the Symbolists only to the extent that other worlds could be perceived through it, and therefore they diminished the intrinsic worth of the actual world.   The Acmeists, on the contrary, respected the world for its own sake.   ". . .The rose became good again by itself. . ." for its petals, scent, and color. The beauty of the rose was an end in itself, a satisfactory perceptual object, not having to symbolize something higher.[66] Gorodeckij felt that the Acmeists expressed a love for the world in their poetry, a love evident in the exoticism of Gumilev and in the "Adamism" of Zenkevič and Narbut.   The poet had become a "new Adam," the original perceiver, for whom the entire world was a new and exciting theme.[67]   Gorodeckij's reiteration of Gumilev's ideas probably represents an attempt to "jump on the bandwagon" of the new movement currently in fashion, a trait that would later lead him to denounce Acmeism.

Mandel'štam's "Utro Akmeizma" ("The Morning of Acmeism") was far more sophisticated and to the point than the essays of either Gumilev or Gorodeckij in formulating the aesthetic theories and directions of the new school.[68] Although the essay did not appear until 1919 in the Voronež miscellany *Sirena* (*The Siren*), it nevertheless had the characteristics of an Acmeist manifesto. Indeed the critic N. K. Xardžiev has tentatively established that "The Morning of Acmeism," written in 1912, was to have been printed with Gumilev's and Gorodeckij's manifestoes in the number 1, 1913 issue of *Apollon*. Mandel'štam's references to Symbolism date this essay from 1912 rather than 1919. "Morning" refers not only to the beginnings of a literary movement, but also to the clarity, freshness, and brilliance for which a good deal of Acmeist poetry, particularly that of Axmatova and Mandel'štam, is known.[69] There is, in addition, an association with light, the visual image, clear perception and, ultimately, linearity, all of these components of Acmeism.

Mandel'štam differed from Gumilev and Gorodeckij in making no references to the possible decline or demise of Symbolism, limiting himself to criticizing only those aspects of Symbolism antithetical to Acmeism. Unlike his fellow theoreticians, he relegated the world view of the artist (as expressed in his art) to a secondary position, emphasizing that form was his primary consideration. For the artist, he stated, the world view is an instrument, like "a hammer in the hands of a stonemason, and the only reality is the work itself."[70] It would appear at first glance that Mandel'štam did not posit art as a centralizing substitute for lost values, but this is not, in fact, the case. It is in this very emphasis on form that Mandel'štam both defines art as formal construction and simultaneously places it at the center of history.

Stressing that the word was the building block of poetry, Mandel'štam declared that ". . .reality in poetry is the word as such. . . ." In expository prose, he continued, one spoke essentially with consciousness, not the word. The word had to be intrinsically significant, not acquiring its importance from the ideas it conveyed. The concept of "the word as such" was slow in developing. All other elements of it except for the conscious sense, or Logos, were included in the concept of form. The Logos is still arbitrarily and mistakenly thought of as the content of the word, but Logos needs only to be on an equal basis with the other elements of the word. Mandel'štam quarreled with the Futurists who could not cope, he felt, with the conscious sense of the word as creative material and therefore discarded it; in this way, the Futurist repeated the "crude mistake of his forebears." For the Acmeists, stated Mandel'štam, the conscious sense of the word or the Logos was as beautiful a form as music was for the Symbolists. In ignoring or discarding the conscious sense of the word, the Futurists robbed it of its dignity. Under the Acmeists, however, the word had entered the first stages of its evolution.[71]

Mandel'štam opposed the Acmeist poet-builder's sharp pleasure in craftsmanship to the "sting of decadence" (of the Symbolists) and to the Futurists' delight in form devoid of conscious sense. The Acmeists do not "renounce. . .their own gravity, but joyously accept it in order to awaken and use the forces architecturally sleeping in it." Mandel'štam's comparison of the (Acmeist) poet with the architect underscores the visual, structural, and spatial emphases of the movement. The architectural form dearest to him was the cathedral, with its joint associations with structure and tradition. ". . .We are introducing the Gothic into the relationship of words, just as Sebastian Bach established it in music." Mandel'štam's reference to Bach re-emphasizes his stress on structure and its primal role in art.[72] Surely Bach's compositions, considered in the light of their complex structures, can be considered "musical cathedrals."

His only direct reference to the mysticism of the later Symbolists was a brief one. "The Symbolists," he affirmed, "were bad stay-at-homes, they liked to travel. . . ." They did not "feel at home in the closet of their own organisms and in that world closet that Kant built with the aid of his categories." Mandel'štam realized that the Symbolists were unable to accept the limitations of their earthly existences and endeavored to use poetry as a means of transcending reality.

He himself, however, did not try to escape his surroundings.

> "In order to build successfully, the first condition is a true piety for the three dimensions of space—to look at them, not as a burden or an unfortunate accident, but as a palace given by God. . . It is possible to build only in the name of the 'three dimensions,' since they are the condition of all architecture. That is why the

architect must be a good stay-at-home, but the Symbolists were bad architects. To build means to struggle with emptiness."[73]

The later Symbolists, he added, refused to work within the limitations of the human condition and attempted to escape from it into a world beyond their own material one. Their rejection of the "three dimensions" of their world resulted in a similar and related neglect of literary form, the artistic parallel to it, with form merely an instrument for attempting to attain an exterior goal.

The Acmeists' acceptance of the "three dimensions" was expressed in part in their "love of the organism," which Mandel'štam believes them to have shared with the "physiologically brilliant Middle Ages." Notre Dame was a "festival of physiology," an assertion of man's ability to transform the "empty spaces" of the universe into comprehensible "aesthetic solidity." He criticized the nineteenth century (the Romantics and Symbolists) for having lost the secret of true complexity that exists necessarily within the bounds of the physical world.[74] It was these writers who had instead sought a false complexity beyond the bounds of the "three dimensions."

While Gumilev argued that the Acmeists were aesthetic descendants of such earlier masters as Rabelais and Shakespeare, he never formulated a hypothesis for placing the Acmeists within such a context. It was left to Mandel'štam to go beyond the mere statement of a superficial, practical doctrine to posit a theoretical basis for the movement. "Love the existence of the thing more than the thing itself and your own existence more than yourself—that is the highest commandment of Acmeism," he asserted.[75] Mandel'štam's cryptic command must be viewed as the basis for Acmeism. Loving the "existence of the thing more than the thing itself" stresses that each atomized individual has value, indeed significance, only insofar as it exists as a part of a great whole, in this instance, as a part of a chain of existence, specifically as a link in the overall structure of civilization. This chain of existence was synonymous, in Mandel'štam's hypothesis, with the three dimensions of existence. It was a structure representing the only alternative to the chaos to which the Symbolists were drawn, the chaos that the Futurists would attempt to dominate. When the Symbolists allowed themselves to be atomized in their stress on the transcending consciousness of the individual artist, they severed themselves from the chain that represented the only bulwark between themselves and the abyss, and they were lost.

Mandel'štam viewed the logic of Acmeism as a further link in the chain and contrasted it to the alogic of Symbolism:

"A=A: What a splendid poetic theme. Symbolism languished, was bored by the law of identity: Acmeism makes a slogan of it and offers it instead of the doubtful *a realibus ad realiora.*"[76]

"A=A," the "law of identity," is the logical link between the fact of existence and existence itself, the equation of each thing with its place along the chain, within the temporal and linear constructs with which the human mind defines the world outside itself. It is by these means that Mandel'štam sought to define both space and time as structural alternatives to emptiness. The Symbolists, who loved the self more than the existence of the self and attempted to define a state beyond what could normally be conceived of, lacked the ability and desire to accept the equation between the existence of the individual and the individual itself. They preferred to identify themselves with the amorphous, unknowable realms beyond the normal boundaries of existence. But the Acmeists accepted this equation. This is the clarity to which Kuzmin alluded but never defined. It was left to Annenskij, with his muse holding the measuring triad delimiting the three dimensions, with the poet in his metapoetry existing within a context, a chain of poets in a linear world, to define it. It is the poet, insisted Mandel'štam, who regards the law of identity with "reverential wonder." Logic "is the kingdom of unexpectedness. . . A logical connection for us is not the tune about the siskin, but a symphony with an organ and singing. . . ." And Mandel'štam added a reference to the architect of music, Bach.[77] Mandel'štam regarded Bach's music rather as an interplay of linear structures than as simple melodies, and he removed it from its normal context of sound to place it within a visual, structural context. Mandel'štam's assertion that "We do not fly; we ascend only those towers which we ourselves can build"[78] stresses yet again that the Acmeists functioned within the linearity of the three dimensions, symbolized again by architecture, beyond which lay the abyss into which the mind could not attempt to penetrate, for this very penetration spelled the death of civilization.

In his last paragraph, Mandel'štam criticized the Symbolists,

contrasting them unfavorably with the artists of the Middle Ages.
The Middle Ages:

> "Never mixed the various planes and treated the beyond
> with enormous restraint.   The noble mixture of
> rationality and mysticism and the perception of the
> world as a living equilibrium relates us to this epoch
> and impels [us] to draw strength from works that arose
> on Romance soil about the year 1200."[79]

Mandel'štam might seem to be suggesting here that the
Acmeists themselves subscribed to mysticism, but this is not the
case.   The "noble mixture" is an equivalent of the statement that
the artists of the Middle Ages ". . .never mixed the various planes
and treated the beyond with enormous restraint."   "Noble" means
"balanced," "careful," "discriminating."   The Acmeists, he suggests,
like the architects of the Middle Ages, were able to achieve an
equilibrium between mysticism (here meaning awareness, but not
comprehension, of the unknown) and rationality (comprehension
and acceptance of the three dimensions).   Mandel'štam's reference
to the cathedral solidifies the ideas of this paragraph, since the bell
towers of the cathedral represent the zenith of the artist's
transformation of the three dimensions.   Physically, spiritually, and
aesthetically, it is the point at which man penetrates space and
touches the beyond; it demonstrates the mental molding of
perception.

Mandel'štam concluded "The Morning of Acmeism" as follows:

> "We shall prove our rightness in such a way that in
> response to us the entire chain of causes and effects
> from alpha to omega will shudder; we shall learn to
> bear more easily and freely the mobile fetters of
> existence."[80]

This sentence can be understood more readily if its two
clauses are reversed. In the second one, Mandel'štam signified that
the Acmeists ("we") would learn to accept the limitations ("mobile
fetters") of the three dimensions in which they live. "Bear more
easily and freely" refers to the artist's freedom to create formal
beauty within the boundaries of the three dimensions. The beauty
the Acmeists would create, he declared, would be of tremendous
importance. Like the artists of the Middle Ages, they would have
accepted the position of man and art within a finite framework and
could then channel their energies and talents into the creation of

beauiful form. They could create a lasting art similar to that of
the Middle Ages, an art that would startle the world by its very
significance. An art of this importance, enduring art, would take
its place in the great chain of civilization, a chain representing the
ability of the mind to transform perception into art.

Mandel'štam's essay owes its comparatively greater significance
to his specific definition of the aesthetic theories of the new literary
school. He did not try to subordinate art to doctrine, a mistake
made by both Gumilev and Gorodeckij. He did not attempt to
mold aesthetics to fit the specific model of Acmeism, but conceived
of Acmeism as part of a larger system of aesthetics, even of
metaphysics itself, and, for him, this was its overriding virtue.

CONCLUSION

In spite of the glibness, carelessness, and superficiality that
may have marred Gumilev's "The Precepts of Symbolism, and
Acmeism" and Gorodeckij's "Some Tendencies in Contemporary
Russian Poetry," their essays nevertheless mark a definitive break
with Symbolism in both aesthetic values and world view. The
most significant feature of all three essays was their establishment
of a new focus for poetry. The Symbolists placed the artist at the
center of his work, a practice reflected in their use of suggestion
through symbols (implying that the artist alone could understand
his poem definitively), in their mysticism (the poet could escape his
earthly limitations through art, the ultimate development from the
use of suggestion), and in their use of abstractions (a stylistic
counterpart to mysticism, and a parallel to the use of suggestion).

The artist occupied a place of secondary importance for the
Acmeists, particularly for Mandel'štam. The significance of the
artist lay in an ability to transform the immediate, material world
into beautiful form, art. The work of art, not the artist, was at
the center. Gumilev's conception of man as a phenomenon among
phenomena and his condemnation of mysticism as a prostitution of
art illustrates this, as does Gorodeckij's emphasis on the primacy of
beauty in his argument that the rose was significant for its own
sake.

By insisting on the irrefutable and cardinal centrality of art,
Mandel'štam went further than either Gumilev or Gorodeckij. The
artist acquired significance only through what he had produced. It
was not only Symbolism that Mandel'štam rejected; he went on to

condemn all art in which perfection of form was secondary to other factors and in which man's relationship to art was lacking or misunderstood. (He was generally critical of the art of the nineteenth century.) Mandel'štam believed that Acmeism could and indeed must continue the tradition important in the Middle Ages, holding that art should be an integral part of society, of the chain of civilization, within man's physical and intellectual reach, the pinnacle of rational creativity and mechanical practicality. Mandel'štam strongly and fundamentally criticized the breakdown of an accepted role for aesthetics, the disintegration of the chain, which began with the loss of unquestioning belief following the Middle Ages, culminating in the mystical excesses of the later Symbolists. It signified the loss of a center, with the Symbolists and Futurists representing centrifugal, destructive forces.

The Acmeists not only defined a center for poetry; they decided further that art was not a monolith, that the aesthetics of Symbolism in fact represented a false path inimical to art. Although the Acmeists may have espoused ideas publicized earlier by the "clarist" Kuzmin, they went beyond him in consciously breaking with the Symbolist movement and in redefining the relative positions of the poet and poetry. The specifics of the relationship between the Acmeists and Annenskij, considered in terms of their literary doctrine and his aesthetic and world views, will be the focus of the concluding chapter.

CHAPTER SIX

THE LINK BETWEEN
ANNENSKIJ AND ACMEISM

Why were the Acmeists attracted to Annenskij, and why in turn did Annenskij, who normally held himself aloof from all literary entanglements, allow himself to be drawn into their circle?[1] These questions can be answered more readily if we first discuss the physical circumstances making the link possible, returning thereafter to the conclusions of the preceding chapters that have provided the basis for our analysis.

Annenskij became acquainted with the future Acmeists at Tsarskoe Selo (Tsar's Village), where he was named director of the lyceum in 1896. He held this post until 1906, when he was removed from his position for having shielded several older students who had taken part in political disturbances growing out of the 1905 Revolution. His action demonstrated an awareness that the contemporary political system was morally unjustifiable. Following his dismissal from the lyceum, he was made inspector of the St. Petersburg educational district, an exhausting and stressful occupation that undoubtedly hastened his death late in 1909.[2]

Because Puškin and a number of poets from his circle attended the lyceum at Tsarskoe Selo early in the nineteenth century, it is associated with his verse and spirit; Axmatova writes of the "swarthy youth" haunting the grounds, a young poet carrying a volume of Parny.[3] The school itself was a liberal establishment for that time; Greek was not offered, but Russian and French were emphasized. Discipline was not too strict; the school, in Puškin's time, was a pleasant, cultivated institution at which the students could obtain a polished, but not overly strenuous education, and where they could establish enduring relationships.[4] It is linked in the minds of educated Russians with Puškin, with political and cultural liberalism, and with Western culture, particularly that of the French. Given his orientation toward French culture and his enlightened ideas about education, Annenskij was the ideal head for such a school.

In 1903, when Annenskij was the director, Gumilev enrolled in the seventh class.[5] It was a fateful meeting for the further development of Russian literature. The closeness of their relationship is open to question, yet the memoirist Jurij Annenkov maintains that Annenskij's impact on Gumilev's early verse is readily apparent.[6] Gumilev in fact dedicated several poems to Annenskij and read his early verse aloud "timidly" in Annenskij's office.[7]

Following his return from France in 1908, Gumilev sought Annenskij out and was a frequent visitor in his home.[8] Through Gumilev, his former student, Annenskij gained entry into the literary world of St. Petersburg. Along with Brjusov and Aleksej Nikolaevič Tolstoj, he was a host for Gumilev's group "Akademija stixa" ("The Academy of Verse"), later to be the nucleus of the "Obščestvo revnitelej xudožestvennogo slova" ("Society of the Partisans of the Artistic Word").[9] Gumilev was responsible for Annenskij's initial meeting with Sergej Makovskij, future editor of *Apollon.*[10]

Annenskij had an important role in the affairs of *Apollon* when it was first launched, and it was here that he published several poems and some of his most significant critical essays.[11] *Apollon* in its turn paid homage to Annenskij in an anonymous eulogy, presumably by the editor, Makovskij. The author of the eulogy noted Annenskij's youthful orientation, erudition, brilliant mind, and responsive personality, characterizing the older man as one of the "best representatives of Russian culture" of his time.[12]

Although Annenskij had published essays in *The Journal of the Ministry of Public Education* and *The Russian School*, both of these were pedagogical rather than literary journals. A major literary organ of this same period, *Vesy* (*The Scales*, which ceased publication in 1910) was clearly Symbolist and, since Annenskij avoided literary alliances with this school, he would have been drawn instead to an unaligned publication. *Apollon* was not initially an Acmeist journal (the essays comprising the Acmeist doctrine did not appear there for four years following its inception). Arguments among members of the various Symbolist factions "graced" its pages, a situation symbolizing the state of flux in contemporary Russian letters. Yet it was clearly a publication of classical intent and style, an orientation evident from its name.

Apollon was the only feasible outlet for Annenskij's work at this time, and it was indeed fortuitous that he was able to gain access to it through Gumilev.

Gumilev was the self-conscious founder of a new literary movement, aware that his pronouncements would attract attention. Having designated four writers of the past (Shakespeare, Rabelais, Villon, and Gautier) who would serve as anchors for his venture, he needed a contemporary, living author to furnish a sense of legitimacy for the future. What better choice than Annenskij, the non-aligned, self-effacing teacher, separate from the Symbolists and sympathetic to new literary currents? Annenskij, translator of the Parnassians and French Symbolists in *Parnascy i prokljatye* (*The Parnassians and the Accursed Ones* [The Symbolists]) was "tuned in" to the "Romanic" world as opposed to the "Germanic" one, and Gumilev considered Romanic culture crucial for the Acmeists.

Gumilev regarded Annenskij not only as a Russian poet, but as a writer of European stature as well. With Annenskij's death, wrote Gumilev, not only Russia but "all Europe lost one of [its] greatest poets."[13] The Acmeists' preference for the literature of Western Europe might well have been due at least in part to their closeness to Annenskij, and Gumilev probably learned about the Parnassians and the French Symbolists through his teacher.[14] Both Annenskij and the Acmeists were attracted to and influenced by the aesthetic values of the Parnassians: as an element of poetic expression, the word possessed intrinsic worth, clarity was to be stressed, the values of the past were to be preserved, poetry was to be considered a craft and the poet a craftsman.[15] An acceptance of the three-dimensional world and rejection of the mysticism peculiar to the younger Symbolists ran parallel to Annenskij's and the Acmeists' conception of the poet as craftsman and to their emphasis on clarity and the word. Having examined Annenskij's verse from the vantage point of thematics, we can readily see that his work illustrates his aesthetic theories.

Annenskij's relationship with Gumilev was somewhat uneven, however. As a result, some critics have maintained that the two were not really close as poets, hypothesizing further that, with Gumilev considered the central figure in the movement, Annenskij's poetry had little in common with Acmeist verse.[16] Shortly before his execution in 1921, Gumilev told his fellow Acmeist Georgij Adamovič that Annenskij was an "insignificant" poet who did not have true creative energy; Gumilev thus repudiated his previous

positive assessments of Annenskij's poetic talents.   Adamovič
reacted cautiously, suggesting that Gumilev may have been jealous
of Annenskij's following among younger poets and that Gumilev, as
head of a literary school, wanted to be considered the final
authority on poetic questions.[17]   It is well to remember, moreover,
that Gumilev's tie with Annenskij enabled the latter to gain access
to *Apollon.*   Equally significant, it was through Gumilev that he
met Axmatova and Mandel'štam.

Anna Axmatova's family moved to Tsarskoe Selo in 1890, the
year after her birth, and she made her first contact with Annenskij
through Gumilev, when she was still a student.[18] Axmatova had
enormous respect for Annenskij, considering him extremely
important for later developments in twentieth-century Russian
poetry. He represented simultaneously a link with the culture of
the past and a bridge to the future. Enthralled by the poems in
Kiparisovyj larec (*The Cypress Chest*), she read them "having
forgotten everything else in the world."[19] She termed Annenskij "a
mighty poet" from whom "everyone emerged."[20]   So important was
he for her stylistically that she has even been called his "direct
heiress."[21]   She shared with Annenskij a preference for a
superficially simple, elegant style, the use of a central mood in a
poem, and an abiding respect for art. Both poets employed a
persona and conversational elements in their verse. Her enthusiasm
for the older poet may well have triggered Gumilev's jealousy and
could have been a factor in his later, fleeting disenchantment with
his former teacher. But neither Gumilev, despite his position of
leadership, his echo Gorodeckij, nor Axmatova was the central
theoretician of Acmeism. That was Mandel'štam.

Mandel'štam lived in Pavlovsk, near Tsarskoe Selo, and knew
Annenskij well. He shared in the general, local interest in
Puškin.[22]   A convert to Russian Orthodoxy, Mandel'štam saw
himself as a bridge between the culture of the past, on which he
drew, and the developments of the future. He shared Axmatova's
high regard for Annenskij. Mandel'štam declared in his essay "O
prirode slova" ("On the Nature of the Word") that Annenskij was
unique in the literature of his time, an unusual poet with no
parallel before or since who had made at least some contribution to
Western culture with his work on Euripides.[23]   Mandel'štam
considered Annenskij the only contemporary poet conversant with
the cultures of the past. He felt that Annenskij had had an
enormous impact on Russian verse, and Mandel'štam considered

him to be the first teacher of psychological keenness in contemporary Russian poetry, a poet without equal in his time.[24]

As can be seen in Chapter Two, Annenskij's verse can be divided according to six major themes: death, life, dream, nature, time, and art. Time is the primary theme dominating all others save art. For Annenskij, time can be neither surmounted nor avoided. It is eternally, inescapably present, as in the lyric "Stal'naja cikada" ("The Steel Cicada"), one of his most complex poems. Annenskij's acknowledgement of the power of time underscores his acceptance of the three-dimensional world that the early Symbolists ignored and the later ones rejected. It was precisely in their attempt to escape from time that the Symbolists sought first to avoid and eventually to sever the flow of historical development. The Futurists' rejection of past culture also equals a rejection of time. It was this world of physical reality, essential for cultural achievement, that both Annenskij and the Acmeists sought to preserve.

Annenskij positioned time and art at two ends of a scale. Art counterweighted time as the only enduring entity. This juxtaposition was to find an echo in Mandel'štam's "The Morning of Acmeism," where the author emphasized that the artist's acceptance of the three dimensions of existence was a prerequisite to the creative act, criticizing the later Symbolists for their disregard of earthly existence and quest for escape. If we return to Chapter One and an earlier discussion of the Acmeists, we can see that time has a contradictory role not only as the vehicle of destruction, but also as the medium through which art can endure. We can find the impetus for Mandel'štam's views in Annenskij's verse. Time conquers the individual artist (the singer in "After the Concert") but is powerless against the statue of Puškin ("The Bronze Poet"). Annenskij was immersed inescapably in the actual world, and he cried out in frustration against devouring time in "The Steel Cicada" and "Nocturno." But Annenskij also knew that art was an independent force, and in "The Bronze Poet" his poet conquered time. The choice of a statue of Puškin is no accident, for it was Puškin who symbolized the permanence, the power of art for both Annenskij and the Acmeists. Puškin *used* time, tying together the past and the future, skeins from two different continua, the Russian one (his use of folk themes, of prose elements, of the peasant name "Tatjana" in *Eugene Onegin*) and the Western one (the Byronic hero, his mastery of Western writers and forms). It was Puškin who created the ambiance at Tsarskoe Selo and embodied the power and continuity of art. (Again, the Symbolists' avoidance of him and the Futurists' rejection are symptomatic of their cultural disorientation.) It was Annenskij who understood and continued his work, the only figure of modern poetry who linked, in a similar fashion, the past and present, Russia and the West. This was the reason why Axmatova read *The Cypress Chest*, "having forgotten all else." Annenskij, like Puškin, enabled her to merge with time, with her culture.

When the artist perishes but his art survives, the emphasis is on the work itself and the artist is merely a craftsman. Annenskij considered the poet a craftsman of clear verse in such lyrics as "Into the Magic Prism," "The Bronze Poet," and "To the Poet." The prism of the first lyric symbolizes the poet, who transforms the clear light of inspiration into the colors that constitute a work of art. Both Annenskij and the Acmeists equated art with visual perception (music, as seen in the analyses of "After the Concert" or "The Bow and Strings," is ephemeral for Annenskij).[25] This runs counter to the Symbolist emphasis on sound (especially true of Aleksandr Blok) but dovetails with the conception of art and time discussed above. Sound is lost (the notes in the grass in "After the Concert"), but the plastic arts endure (the statue in "The Bronze Poet").

In "Drugomu" ("To Another"), Annenskij contrasts himself to the Symbolist poet, whom he designates a "god" while he himself is only a "moralist," an interpreter lacking absolute authority. He identifies the veiled goddess Isis as the Symbolist muse in "To the Poet," while simultaneously aligning himself with the clear art and visual orientation characterizing the art of classical Greece. Annenskij, wrote Setchkarev, insisted on "the objective, concrete conciseness of his own poetry" as opposed to the "sweet airiness" of Symbolist verse.[26] He was firmly within the confines of the physical world, divorced from the mysticism of the later Symbolists. The differences between Annenskij and the Symbolists and, eventually and by extension, between the Symbolists and Acmeists, were expressed aesthetically, but the basis for these differences was ultimately philosophical in nature. The Symbolists' initial employment of suggestion and the symbol eventually and indeed inevitably developed into using of art to furnish a framework, to fill the void left by the rapid collapse of the social structure prior to the 1917 revolutions.

The Symbolists not only sought and, eventually, found their final answer, they even bestowed a label upon it, Sophia. Their use of sound to attempt to "catch" signals from the other worlds, ultimate worlds, into which they tried to penetrate, is symptomatic of their separation from the physicality of the actual world. Annenskij, on the other hand, used the visual image rather than the aural; even in "Poetry," the signs of poetry are seen (the traces of her sandals in the sand) rather than heard. As seen in Chapters Two and Three, his was a world limited by the clouds, defined by intersecting planes in space, and by rays of light that define these planes. Because he considered the artist an individual who intercepted phenomena to create art, we can separate him definitively from the Symbolists and link him instead with the Acmeists, who considered it impossible for the poet to divorce himself from the phenomena that he could literally perceive.

Annenskij's conception of the poet as craftsman is linked to his rejection of the later Symbolists' position that the poet was primarily a seer and art religion.[27]   A. Fedorov felt that the Symbolists adopted poses, while the hero of Annenskij's poems was a simple poetic "I."[28]   As Axmatova was to do later, Annenskij conceived of the poetic narrator as distinct from the poet himself; in some cases, this persona can be considered the protagonist of the lyric.[29]   By establishing a space between writer and persona, Annenskij emphasized the work itself rather than the writer and placed that work firmly within the confines of actuality. This constitutes a rejection of the Symbolist view that the work of art provides a means of escaping from the physical world and stresses, in addition, the autonomous position of art.

The Acmeists agreed with Annenskij in regarding the poet as a craftsman and poetry as a craft; Mandel'štam considered him an architect-builder.[30]   Mandel'štam's pairing of the poet and architect is central to his conception of Acmeism. First of all, he linked the poet with the visual, plastic arts (as did Annenskij in "The Bronze Poet") rather than with music. He identified the poet specifically with the architect-engineer of the Middle Ages. In both Eastern and Western Europe, the architecture of the Middle Ages was the architecture of the church. The very gradual evolution of the arts, society, and religion during this period produced a sensation of static time, of timelessness. This was an age of stability when the artist was integrated into the larger world, with his work of art a part of the larger cultural milieu.

The greatest art of this period in the West, the Gothic cathedral, is based on a stressing of the vertical rather than the horizontal, on the achievement of linear thrust that is both physically overwhelming and temporally static. Space was subordinated to structure. The Middle Ages were a very attractive period for Mandel'štam. He was fundamentally disturbed by the constant disruptions synonymous with modernism, disruptions that splintered the normal flow of time and threatened the continuity of culture.

The cathedral, moreover, was a symmetrical structure, forming perfectly balanced halves of a cross, and the basis for construction was the straight line, with a pointed rather than a rounded arch. We have seen these same lines in Annenskij's poetry, specifically in "To the Poet," "Poetry," and "Into the Magic Prism." This is the cathedral of Mandel'štam's essay.

The construction formed from lines and planes underscores the central importance of clarity in the work of art, and the physical, visual clarity was translated into linguistic clarity. Both Annenskij and the Acmeists stressed clarity of expression, advocating the use of colloquialisms (conversational elements) in verse and images that were concrete rather than abstract.[31] Annenskij's diction was "studiously common and trivial. . .the uncommon language of the everyday. . . ."[32] It was direct, perhaps linear language. Even Annenskij's nature lyrics contained prosaisms, and the combination of the structure of the traditional nature poem with discordant stylistic elements alters the traditional result and shocks the reader.[33] Prosaisms set the work within the framework of the everyday world, a world identified with objects, with visual images, with time. It is an immediate physical world, a concrete world opposed to the realm of mystical correspondences inhabited by the later Symbolists. The use of colloquial language and the concomitant stress on the "word as such" points to a logical basis for art, art that is part of a rational system.[34] Annenskij considered the writing of verse as founded on a rational basis.[35] He regarded poetic composition as primarily an intellectual exercise based on the logical use of words, and Mandel'štam, in "The Morning of Acmeism," stressed the importance of logic in verse and asserted that logic was a component of the highest achievements in art.[36]

Annenskij did not rely upon prosaic, conversational elements

alone to produce concrete images. He used personification to
identify the outside world that he could perceive with the mind
and its role in interpreting sensation. Nowhere is this better
illustrated than in "The Bow and Strings," with its vivid
reproduction of tactile sensation and with the components of an
instrument brought to life as lovers. Personification underscores
the physical reality of the poetic setting, providing a marked
contrast to abstraction. The Acmeists may well have found a
justification for their "cult of things," their acceptance of the
physical world, in the person and work of Annenskij.[37]

Annenskij anticipated the Acmeists not only in his poetic
themes and techniques, but in his literary criticism as well. He
was a "defender of pure form in art," a poet for whom art was no
more than a representation of reality.[38] The Acmeists seconded
this view in their insistence on the autonomy of art and the
significance of aesthetic form. They followed Annenskij's lead in
respecting the word as the fundamental unit of poetry. Annenskij
thought the word "aesthetically valuable," regarding it as the basic
component of a poem.[39] For the Acmeists, particularly
Mandel'štam, the "word as such" was "reality in poetry."[40]
Mandel'štam attached the same degree of importance to the word
that the other Acmeist theoreticians, Gumilev and Gorodeckij,
placed upon the world of discrete phenomena.

Annenskij regarded poetry as "the highest manifestation of the
creative power of speech," considering it impossible to know a
language without having mastered its poetry or to know poetry
without in turn knowing the language.[41] In "The Precepts of
Symbolism, and Acmeism," Gumilev also stressed the importance of
"living speech" in poetry.[42] The connection between speech and
poetry is yet another manifestation of the emphasis on form and
on a rational, actual basis for poetry.

CONCLUSION

The Acmeists considered themselves within the stream of
historical development, refusing either to escape from it, as did the
Symbolists, or to repudiate it, as the Futurists were to do.
Annenskij was the sole contemporary Russian poet who could serve
as a model for Acmeism. He alone grasped the significance of the
cultural achievements of Russia and the West, both past
achievements and contemporary ones. He knew that the

preservation of civilization was crucial, viewing art as the only means for overcoming temporal limitations to merge with the linear thrust of civilization. Both Annenskij and the Acmeists considered art visual expression that could evolve into structure, specifically, linear structure or architecture, particularly in the case of Mandel'štam. What better symbol for both the physicality and the enormous significance of art as emblematic of civilization than the medieval cathedral, the cathedral in "The Morning of Acmeism," in the lyrics "Notre Dame" and "Hagia Sophia?"

An analysis of the relationship between Annenskij and the Acmeists is crucial for understanding Russian poetry during the Silver Age of Modernism. Even more important, the link between them is but one link in an entire chain of the evolution of Russian literature. It is an evolution with definite peaks, one of which is the brilliant phenomenon of Puškin's work at the beginning of the nineteenth century. Puškin's role was as interlocutor between Russia and the West, between earlier aesthetic values and the later development of Russian literature. Annenskij and the Acmeists, who understood and respected the basis for Puškin's contribution, are another peak in this evolution. Together they demonstrate that the spirit of civilization so revered by Puškin was capable of survival into the twentieth century.

APPENDIX

The concepts that the Acmeists espoused in the essays comprising their doctrine were incorporated into their verse as well. A brief examination of the lyrics of the three principal Acmeist poets, Anna Axmatova, Nikolaj Gumilev, and Osip Mandel'štam, will demonstrate the closeness of the poems under consideration to points made in the essays and, by extension, to the aesthetic values of Annenskij.

Conversational elements anchor lyrics within the everyday world. They occur frequently in Axmatova's poems. In "Sžala ruki pod temnoj vual'ju" ("I Squeezed [Wrung] my Hands Under a Dark Veil"], fragments of conversation form a dialogue between the persona and other voices in the poem. The exchange results in a tight little drama clearly placed within the confines of the everyday world, yet unmistakably separated from it by the strictures of form.

> "Sžala ruki pod temnoj vual'ju. . .
>   'Otčego ty segodnja bledna?'
>   – Ottogo, čto ja terpkoj pečal'ju
>   Napoila ego dop'jana.
>
> Kak zabudu? On vyšel, šatajas',
> Iskrivilsja mučitel'no rot. . .
> Ja sbežala, peril ne kasajas',
> Ja bežala za nim do vorot.
>
> Zadyxajas', ja kriknula: 'Šutka
> Vse, čto bylo. Ujdeš', ja umru.'
> Ulybnulsja spokojno i žutko
> I skazal mne: 'Ne stoj na vetru.'"[1]

> "I wrung my hands under the dark veil. . .
>   'Why are you so pale today?'
>   – Because I made him drunk
>   With astringent sadness.
>
> How shall I forget? He left, reeling,
> Distorting his mouth poignantly. . .

I ran out, not touching the railings,
I ran after him to the gate.
Choking, I shouted: 'Everything that happened was a joke.
If you leave, I'll die.'
He smiled quietly and horribly
And told me: 'Don't stand in the wind.'"

This is a playlet with three characters, the persona, her confidante, and the man who has run out the door. The circumstances causing the breach are not clarified, yet the significance of the lyric is rather in the expression of the tensions among the three voices, particularly the voices of the persona and the man. Axmatova creates dialogue where a lesser poet would have settled for monologue; in the last line, "otvetil" ("answered") could have been substituted for "Skazal mne" ("Told me") with no real change in metrics or semantics, yet "skazal mne" contains an interlocutor as well as a speaker, while "otvetil" does not.

The figure of "Poetry" in Annenskij's lyric of that name, who has given the poet instructions on how to write verse, has become the more conventional, intimate "Muse" of Axmatova's "Muza" ("The Muse"). She enters the persona's own world.

"Kogda ja noc'ju ždu ee prixoda,
Žizn', kažetsja, visit na voloske,
Čto počesti, čto junost', čto svoboda
Pred miloj gost'ej s dudočkoj v ruke.
I vot vošla. Otkinuv pokryvalo,
Vnimatel'no vzgljanula na menja.
Ej govorju: 'Ty l' Dantu diktovala
Stranicy Ada?' Otvečaet: 'Ja.'"[2]

"When I await her coming during the night,
Life, it seems, hangs by a slender thread.
What are honors, what are youth, what are freedom
Before the dear guest with a pipe in her hand.
And now she has come. Having thrown off her shawl [veil],
She glanced attentively at me.
I say to her: 'Didst thou dictate the pages
Of *The Inferno* to Dante?' She responds: 'I.'"

This dialogue is between the persona and her muse. She is

not unique to the persona, but is the muse who has inspired great poets of the past, in this case Dante, one of Axmatova's favorites. What is the significance of Dante for Axmatova? She studied and translated him during a period when it was extremely difficult for her to publish her own verse. He represents the accomplishments of Italy, symbol of the high cultural achievement that the Acmeists revered and to which they clung. Dante signifies for Axmatova what the cathedral and Bach represent for Mandel'štam—the inviolability of beautiful structure, the vital necessity of the continuity of civilization. While she may not have written essays that would be part of the Acmeist doctrine, Axmatova nevertheless subscribed in her verse to the tenets of her fellow Acmeists, particularly Mandel'štam.

Like Annenskij, Axmatova emphasized visual perception in her lyrics, and, by extension, stressed the limitations of the physical world. The sky is glass in "Pustyx nebes prozračnoe steklo" ("The Transparent Glass of the Empty Heavens"), an image resembling Annenskij's solidified skies in "Bronzovyj poèt" ("The Bronze Poet").[3] In "Sad" ("The Garden"), the sun in the second stanza is a pale, dim face ("I solnce, blednyj, tusklyj lik") that degenerates in the fourth and last stanza into a dead one ("Sklonilaja tusklyj mertvyj lik").[4] The dim light and the mood of despair are very much like the atmosphere found in Annenskij's work, with the natural world compartmentalized and incorporated into the human one.

Like Annenskij in "Bronzovyj poèt," ("The Bronze Poet"), Axmatova too wrote a lyric about Puškin and Tsarskoe Selo. Her Puškin in the famous "V Tsarskom Sele, Pt. III, Smuglyj otrok brodil po allejam" ("In Tsarskoe Selo, Pt. III, The Swarthy Youth Wandered along the Paths") is a spirit so alive in its natural environs (Tsarskoe Selo) that it has become a living boy.

> "Smuglyj otrok brodil po allejam
> U ozernyx grustil beregov,
> I stoletie my leleem
> Ele slyšnyj šelest šagov.
>
> Igly sosen gusto i kolko
> Ustilajut nizkie pni. . . Zdes' ležala ego treugolka
> I rastrepannyj tom Parni."[5]

"The swarthy youth wandered along the paths

He was sad at the shores of the lake,
And a century later we cherish
The barely audible rustle of his steps.
The pine needles thickly and prickily
Cover the low stumps. . .
Here lay his cocked hat
And a dog-eared volume of Parny."

Puškin is linked both with the culture of the West, especially that of the French (the volume of Parny), and with Russia as well (the beautiful park with its old pines and its lake). So great a writer was he, so successfully did he synthesize Russian and Western art, that his spirit is still alive in his natural habitat, the park at Tsarskoe Selo that itself represents both Russia and the West. It is like the statue in Annenskij's lyric that sprang to life, emblematic of the enduring quality of Puškin's art.

Gumilev's espousal of clarity in his essay "Zavety simvolizma i akmeizm" ("The Precepts of Symbolism, and Acmeism") was expressed in his verse by the use of visual images, particularly those in brilliant color. In "Osennjaja pesnja" ("Autumnal Song"), the following images occur:

"Osennej nagi poceluj
Gorel v lesax zvezdoju aloj
I pesn' prozračno-zvonkix struj
Kazalas' tixoj i ustaloj.

S derev'ev padal list suxoj,
To bledno-želtyj, to bagrjanyj,
Pečal'no plača nad zemlej
Sredi rosistogo tumana."
            [6]

"The kiss of the autumnal bliss
Was burning in the forests like a scarlet star
And the song of the transparent-sonorous streams
Seemed quiet and tired.

A dry leaf was falling from the trees,
Now pale yellow, now crimson,
Sadly crying above the earth
Amid the dewy mist."

It is interesting to note that Gumilev did not always select exotic locales for his lyrics, retaining an interest also in a traditional Russian setting such as this one.

Like Mandel'štam, Gumilev also was drawn to the architecture and the cultural achievements of the West, an interest evident in "Piza" ("Pisa").

> "Solnce žžet vysokie steny,
> Kryši, ploščadi i bazary.
> O, jantarnyj mramor Sieny
> I moločno-belyj Karrary!"[7]

> "The sun is burning the high walls,
> The roofs, the squares, the bazaars.
> O, amber marble of Siena
> And milky-white [marble] of Carrara!"

Gumilev combines brilliant colors with three-dimensional structure in this lyric, producing a sense of perceptible solidity akin to that of the Puškin statue in Annenskij's "Bronzovyj poèt" ("The Bronze Poet"). There is a sense here that the significance of culture is sufficiently great for it to achieve and be symbolized by mass. Again, Gumilev has set his work within the real, perceptible world.

Mandel'štam, the most sophisticated and intricate of the Acmeist theoreticians, was also the most complex Acmeist poet. His overriding concern with the poet as craftsman, with the visual world, and with the structure of the monuments of civilization is central to his verse as well as to his essays.

Mandel'štam wrote a series of poems set in Petersburg and, eventually, Leningrad, a city that obviously possessed great significance for him. Petersburg is important to Mandel'štam for several crucial reasons: it is a deliberately planned, created city, born of the joint efforts of Russian and Western architects and craftsmen; it is a visual city, beautiful to contemplate, in which symmetrical structure is centrally important. Petersburg, above all, is a hybrid, containing elements of both Western and Russian cultures. While not "organically" Russian like Moscow, but designed instead by Italians (and Scots), Petersburg nonetheless was inhabited by Russians, even if these were westernized Russians. It was more than a city to Mandel'štam; it was the physical, architectural incarnation of his milieu and, ultimately, of his poetry and essays. If Lev Tolstoj found his natural environment at Jasnaja poljana, then Mandel'štam encountered his and, by extension, that of Acmeism as a whole, in Petersburg.

He was endowed with brilliant sensitivity to his surroundings and to the social and political events of his time. Mandel'štam was therefore well aware that the Petersburg he loved, emblematic of the marriage of Western cultural achievement and the Russian spirit, city of Puškin and Annenskij, was doomed under the new order. With the consolidation of their power, the Soviets cut Petersburg off from its Western roots and stripped it of its previous significance as arbiter of Russian culture. Mandel'štam considered this change fatal. He voiced his presentiments of the demise of his culture as early as 1916, in the following poem.

> "V Petropole prozračnom my umrem,
> Gde vlastvuet nad nami Prozerpina.
> My v každom vzdoxe smertnyj vozdux p'em,
> I každyj čas nam smertnaja godina."
> . . . .[8]
> "In transparent Petersburg we shall die,
> Where Proserpine rules over us.
> We drink in fatal air in every breath,
> And every hour is a fatal year for us."
>
> . . . .

Mandel'štam touches on the classical world with his reference to Proserpine, consort to Pluto, the Roman god of death and the underworld. She represents a vanished world in an attenuated city. Petropolis, Greek version of Petersburg, is yet another classical note and symbolizes links with Western culture.

The image of foreboding is more concrete and specific in the following:

> "V Peterburge my sojdemsja snova,
> Slovno solnce my poxoronili v nem,
> I blažennoe, bessmyslennoe slovo
> V pervyj raz proiznesem.
> V černom barxate sovetskoj noči,
> V barxate vsemirnoj pustoty,
> Vsë pojut blažennyx žen rodnye oči,

Vsë cvetut bessmertnye cvety."

. . . .[9]

"We shall gather again in Petersburg,
As if we had buried the sun in it,
And we shall utter the blessed, senseless word
For the first time.

In the black velvet of the Soviet night,
In the velvet of universal emptiness,
The dear eyes of the blessed wives always sing,
The deathless flowers always bloom."

. . . .

The name of the city had been officially changed from Petersburg to Petrograd by November, 1920, when Mandel'štam wrote this lyric, yet it is still Petersburg for him. The buried sun symbolizes the light and warmth of a now dead civilization; the central significance that the visual image held for Mandel'štam is evident here. The black velvet of the Soviet night, reminiscent of the velvet in Annenskij's "Smyčok i struny" ("The Bow and Strings") stands for the death of perception and art and, ultimately, personal annihilation. With the demise of Petersburg comes the death of civilization, the severance of ties to the past and the West. That Mandel'štam regarded the Soviet regime as his antithesis and enemy is both evident and understandable in this verse, for the new system was at least partially successful in destroying those values he deemed significant in "The Morning of Acmeism."

NOTES

PREFACE

[1]Semen Karlinskij, "Veščestvennost' Annenskogo," *Novyj žurnal*, No. 85 (New York: 1966), p. 70.

[2]Thomas Shaw, *The Transliteration of Modern Russian for English-Language Publications* (Madison: The University of Wisconsin Press, 1967), p. 3.

CHAPTER ONE

[1]Donald Fanger states that Čexov, for example, used prose fiction as an instrument of poetic implication. Donald Fanger, "The Russianness of the Nineteenth-Century Novel," Theofanis George Stavrou, ed., *Art and Culture in Nineteenth-Century Russia* (Bloomington: Indiana University Press, 1983), p. 52.

[2]Georgette Donchin, *The Influence of French Symbolism on Russian Poetry* ('S-Gravenhage: Mouton and Company, 1958), p. 119.

[3]*Ibid.*, p. 150; N.E. Krutikova and I.T. Kruk, eds., *Russkaja literatura XX veka. dooktjabr'skij period* (Kiev: Višča škola, 1970), p. 260.

[4]Victor Erlich, *The Double Image: Concepts of the Poet in Slavic Literatures* (Baltimore: The Johns Hopkins Press, 1964), p. 10. For a comparison with the situation in Vienna, see Carl Schorske, *Fin-de-Siècle Vienna: Politics and Culture* (New York: Alfred A. Knopf, 1980), pp. 8-9.

[5]Donchin, *French Symbolism*, p. 110. For Andrej Belyj, "each *word* is *sound* first of all." Andrej Belyj, "Magija slov," *Simvolizm* (Moscow: Russkoe Tovariščestvo, 1910. Reprint Munich: Wilhelm Fink Verlag, 1969), p. 430. Music came to be accepted as the "soul of all the arts." Andrej Belyj, "Princip formy v èstetike," *Simvolizm* (Moscow: Russkoe Tovariščestvo, 1910. Reprint Munich: Wilhelm Fink Verlag, 1969), p. 179. Music assumed cardinal importance for Aleksandr Blok as well. Erlich, *The Double Image*, pp. 101-102.

[6]A case in point is the first-generation Symbolist writer and theoretician Dmitrij Merežkovskij, author of the famous essay "O pričinax upadka i o novyx tečenijax sovremennoj russkoj literatury" ("On the Reasons for [its] Decline and on New Tendencies of Contemporary Russian Literature"), which appeared in 1893. For a discussion of this important work, see Valer'jan Poljanskij, "Social'nye korni russkoj poèzii ot simvolistov do našix dnej," in I.S. Ežov and E.I. Samurin, *Russiaja poèzija XX veka* (Moscow: 1925), p. xi.

[7]Donchin, *French Symbolism*, p. 10.

[8]Krutikova and Kruk, *Russkaja literatura*, p. 259; A. A. Volkov, *Russkaja literatura XX veka. dooktjabr'skij period*, (Moscow: Prosveščenije, 1964) p. 381; Viktor Gofman, "Jazyk simvolistov," *Literaturnoe nasledstvo*, Vol. 27–28 (Moscow; Žurnal'no-gazetnoe ob"edinenie, 1937), pp. 55, 62, 70, 85. See also K.[onstantin] Močul'skij, "Poètičeskoe tvorčestvo Anny Axmatovoj," *Russkaja mysl'*, Nos. 3–4 (Sofia: 1921), p. 186; Viktor Žirmunskij, "Preodolevšie simvolizm," *Russkaja mysl'*, No. 12 (1916), p. 27.

[9]Donchin, *Russian Symbolism*, pp. 166–167; D.S. Mirsky, *A History of Russian Literature. II: After 1881*, edited and abridged by Francis J. Whitfield (New York: Alfred A. Knopf, 1949), p. 431.

[10]Volkov, *Russkaja literatura*, pp. 379, 384.

[11]*Ibid.*, p. 386; Krutikova and Kruk, *Russkaja literatura*, p. 259; Volkov, *Russkaja literatura*, p. 381; Gofman, "Jazyk simvolistov," pp. 55, 62. 70, 85.

[12]Donchin, *French Symbolism*, pp. 26, 89; Andrej Belyj, "Kriticizm i simvolizm," *Simvolizm* (Moscow: Russkoe Tovariščestvo, 1910. Reprint Munich: Wilhelm Fink Verlag, 1969), p. 21; Vladimir Pozner, *Panorama de la Littérature Russe Contemporaine* (Paris: Kra, 1929), p. 152; Konstantin Močul'skij, *Andrej Belyj* (Paris: YMCA Press, 1955) p. 41, 53; Volkov, *Russkaja literatura*, pp. 380–381, 384; Konstantin Močul'skij, *Aleksandr Blok*, (Paris: YMCA Press, 1948) p. 43; Vl. Orlov, "Istorija odnoj 'družby-vraždy,'" in Aleksandr Blok and Andrej Belyj, *Perepiska* (Moscow: 1940. Reprint Munich: Wilhelm Fink Verlag, 1969), p. xvi.

[13]Orlov, "Istorija odnoj 'družby-vraždy,'" p. xi.

[14]Močul'skij, *Aleksandr Blok*, p. 71.

[15]Andrej Belyj, "Blok," *Arabeski* (Moscow: 1911. Reprint Munich: Wilhelm Fink Verlag, 1969), p. 458.

[16]E. Aničkov, *Novaja russkaja poèzija* (Berlin: I.P. Ladyžnikov, 1922. Reprint The Hague: Mouton and Company, 1969), p. 64. Donchin expresses a similar point of view. Donchin, *French Symbolism*, p. 26.

[17]Andrej Belyj, "Na perevale," *Simvolizm* (Moscow: Russkoe Tovariščestvo, 1910. Reprint Munich: Wilhelm Fink Verlag, 1969), p. 243; Žirmunskij, "Preodolevšie simvolizm," p. 26; Aničkov, *Novaja russkaja poèzija*, pp. 65–66; Močul'skij, *Aleksandr Blok*, pp. 39–40, 128; Močul'skij, *Andrej Belyj*, p. 51.

[18]E.I. Šamurin, "Osnovnye tečenija v dorevoljucionnoj russkoj poèzii XX veka," in I.S. Ežov and E.I. Šamurin, *Russkaja poèzija XX veka* (Moscow: 1925), p. xxiv.

[19]Valerij Brjusov, "O 'reči rabskoj,' v zaščitu poèzii," *Apollon*, No. 9 (1910), p. 33.

[20]Vjačeslav Ivanov, "Zavety simvolizma," *Apollon*, No. 8 (1910), p. 16.

[21]Donchin, *French Symbolism*, p. 116.

[22]Valerij Brjusov, "Iskusstvo i literatura RSFSR v èpoxu revoljucii (1917–1922). Včera, segodnja i zavtra russkoj poèzii," *Pečat' i revoljucija*, No. 7 (July, 1922), p. 41.

[23]Andrej Belyj, "Smysl' iskusstva," *Simvolizm* (Moscow: Russkoe Tovariščestvo, 1910. Reprint Munich: Wilhelm Fink Verlag, 1969), p. 225.

[24]Andrej Belyj, "Pesn' žizni," *Arabeski* (Moscow: 1911. Reprint Munich: Wilhelm Fink Verlag, 1969), p. 47.

[25]Andrej Belyj, "Èmblematika smysla," *Simvolizm* (Moscow: Russkoe

Tovarišcestvo, 1910. Reprint Munich: Wilhelm Fink Verlag, 1969), p. 67.

[26]Mocul'skij, *Andrej Belyj*, p. 63.

[27]V. Sajanov, *Ot klassikov k sovremennosti. Kriticeskie stat'i* (Leningrad: Priboj, 1929), pp. 79–80.

[28]Donchin, *French Symbolism*, p. 74.

[29]Volkov, *Russkaja literatura*, p. 415; Aleksej Selivanovskij, "Oktjabr' i dorevoljucionnye poèticeskie školy," in Aleksej Selivanovskij, *Ocerki po istorii russkoj sovetskoj poèzii* (Moscow: Xudožestvennaja literatura, 1936), p. 66.

[30]Vasilij L'vov–Rogacevskij, *Novejšaja russkaja literatura* (3rd edition, Moscow–Leningrad: L.D. Frenkel', 1924), pp. 270–271.

[31]Vladimir Markov, *Russian Futurism: A History* (Berkeley and Los Angeles: University of California Press, 1968), p. 62. Igor'–Severjanin also used newspaper jargon in his verse. See Pozner, *La Littérature Russe*, p. 228.

[32]Markov, *Russian Futurism*, pp. 90, 431–432.

[33]Beverly Whitney Kean discusses the initial corresponding development in the plastic arts in *All the Empty Palaces: The Merchant Patrons of Modern Art in Pre–Revolutionary Russia* (New York: Universe Books, 1983), p. 58.

[34]William E. Harkins, *Dictionary of Russian Literature* (Paterson, New Jersey: Littlefield, Adams, and Company, 1959), p. 127.

[35]L'vov–Rogacevskij, *Novejšaja russkaja literatura*, pp. 270–271.

[36]For a discussion of a fictional treatment of this theme, see Janet Tucker, "A Re-examination of Jurij Oleša's *Envy*," *Slavic and East European Journal*, Vol. 26, No. 1 (Spring, 1982), pp. 56–62.

[37]Markov, *Russian Futurism*, p. 46.

[38]Each of the principal Acmeists retained a cultural tie to the culture of the past. Axmatova and Mandel'štam espoused Orthodoxy, and Gumilev was a royalist.

[39]Samurin, "Osnovnye tecenija," p. xxxiv.

[40]Mixail Kuzmin, "O prekrasnoj jasnosti," *Apollon*, No. 4 (April, 1910), pp. 5–10.

[41]The first two sources given here posit 1855 as the date of birth. B. Varneke, "I.F. Annenskij" [Nekrolog], *Žurnal Ministerstva narodnogo prosveščenija*, No. 3 (1910), p. 37; I.S. Ežov and E.I. Samurin, *Russkaja poèzija XX veka* (Moscow: 1925), pp. 561–562. The date in other sources is 1856: Vsevolod Setchkarev, *Studies in the Life and Work of Innokentij Annenskij* (The Hague: Mouton and Company, 1963), p. 9; A. Fedorov, "Poèticeskoe tvorcestvo Innokentija Annenskogo," in *Innokentij Annenskij, Stixotvorenija i tragedii* (Leningrad: Sovetskij pisatel', 1959), p. 6; Catherine Nebolsine Coulter, *Aspects of the Poetry of Innokentij Annenskij* (New York: Columbia University Master's Essay, 1966), pp. 1–2; and A. Ja. Golovin, *Vstreci i vpecatlenija, Vospominanija xudožnika*, edited by and with the commentary of E.F. Gollerbax (Moscow–Leningrad: Iskusstvo, 1940), p. 154.

[42]Fedorov, "Poèticeskoe tvorcestvo Annenskogo," p. 7. On page five of the above work, Fedorov states that the most complete source for Annenskij's biography is an article by his son, Valentin Krivic, "Innokentij Annenskij po semejnym vospominanijam i rukopisnym materialam," *Literaturnaja mysl'*, No. 3 (1925), pp. 208–255.

[43]Annenskij, a scholar of ancient Greek literature, may also have been referring to the name Odysseus used in his escape from Polyphemus. See

Fedorov, "Poètičeskoe tvorčestvo Annenskogo," p. 15; and V. Il'in, "Innokentij Annenskij i konec Periklova veka Rossii," *Vozroždenie*, No. 166 (Paris: October, 1965), p. 46.

[44]Setchkarev, *Annenskij*, pp. 261–262; Fedorov, "Poètičeskoe tvorčestvo Annenskogo," p. 17.

[45]Setchkarev, *Annenskij*, p. 33.

[46]See Innokentij Annenskij, *Puškin i Tsarskoe Selo* (St. Petersburg: Šumaxer Brothers, 1899; first given as a speech at Tsarskoe Selo, 26 May, 1899), pp. 5, 21. Žukovskij is also linked with Tsarskoe Selo. Marie Maline, *Nicolas Gumilev: Poète et critique acméiste* (Brussels: Palais des Académies, 1964), p. 13.

[47]Setchkarev, *Annenskij*, p. 56; Lubov Alex Shapovaloff, *The Aesthetics and Poetics of Innokentij Annenskij* (Seattle: University of Washington Dissertation, 1968), pp. 267, 333.

[48]William E. Harkins, "Baratynski (or Boratynski), Evgeni Abramovich," *Dictionary of Russian Literature* (Paterson, New Jersey: Littlefield, Adams and Company, 1959), p. 16.

[49]Coulter, *Annenskij*, pp. 35–36.

[50]L.Ja. Ginzburg, *O Lirike* (Moscow–Leningrad: Sovetskij pisatel', 1964), p. 352.

[51]E. Malnina, "Innokentij Annenskij," *Literaturnyj sovremennik*, Nos. 6–7 (1940), p. 213; Fedorov, "Poètičeskoe tvorčestvo Annenskogo," p. 36.

[52]This was in marked contrast to the Symbolist school. See the discussion of Symbolism above.

[53]Innokentij Annenskij, "V doroge," *Stixotvorenija i tragedii*, pp. 74–75; "Kartinka," *Ibid.*, pp. 136–137; "Opjat' v doroge," *Ibid.*, pp. 178–179.

[54]"Ijul'. 2," *Ibid.*, pp. 70–71. For a discussion of Annenskij's poems on socio–political themes, see Malnina, "Annenskij," pp. 210–212.

[55]"Peterburg," *Stixotvorenija i tragedii*, p. 199. For critical commentary on this poem, see Fedorov, "Innokentij Annenskij," p. 13. In an alternate stanza not published with this lyric, he expressed a belief in the certain collapse of the tsarist state. *Ibid.*, pp. 31–32.

[56]A. Evgen'ev, "Stixotvorenija Innokentija Annenskogo," *Literaturnoe obozrenie*, No. 14 (1939), p. 33; A. Fedorov, "Innokentij Annenskij," in *Stixotvorenija Innokentija Annenskogo* (Leningrad: Sovetskij pisatel', 1939), pp. 11–12, 14.

[57]"Starye èstonki," *Stixotvorenija i tragedii*, pp. 216–218. Information concerning this tragedy is taken from *Revoljucija 1905–1907 gg. v nacional'nyx rajonax Rossii* (Moscow: 1955), pp. 377–398, cited by Fedorov in the notes to Innokentij Annenskij, *Stixotvorenija i tragedii*, p. 213. See also the following: Fedorov, "Poètičeskoe tvorčestvo Annenskogo," pp. 33–34; Evgen'ev, "Stixotvorenija Innokentija Annenskogo," p. 34.

[58]In addition to his verses on social and political themes, he also left the rough drafts of poems in prose devoted to these same issues. This material is found in his archives in the folder entitled "'Autopsia' i drugie stixotvorenija v proze."

[59]Fedorov, "Poètičeskoe tvorčestvo Annenskogo," pp. 5–7, 14. The writings of the elder Annenskij clearly display the positivist trends of the 1860s. See Setchkarev, *Annenskij*, p. 10. For Annenskij's own views on his family background, consult F. Fidler, "Innokentij Fedorovoč Annenskij," *Pervye*

literaturnye šagi (Moscow: 1911), p. 171.

[60] Annenskij's concern for justice caused strained relations with his superiors, for he was pushed aside from the directorship of the lyceum at Tsarskoe Selo after having shielded some of the participants of the 1905 Revolution from the authorities. Fedorov, "Poètičeskoe tvorčestvo Annenskogo," pp. 6–7.

[61] Nadežda Mandel'štam emphasized her husband Osip's firm grounding in reality, stating that "Acmeism for Osip Mandel'štam was not only a 'yearning for world culture,' but also the affirmation of an earthly and social source." Nadežda Mandel'štam, *Vospominanija* (New York: Chekhov Publishing House, 1970), p. 280.

[62] L.Ja. Ginzburg, *O lirike* (Moscow–Leningrad: Sovetskij pisatel', 1964), pp. 36, 330, 333.

[63] Johannes Holthusen, *Russische Gegenwartsliteratur. I. 1890–1940. Die literarische Avantgarde* (Bern and Munich: Francke Verlag, 1963), p. 51. George Ivask discusses the relationship between the work of the two writers in "Annenskij und Čechov," *Zeitschrift für slavische Philologie*, XXVII (1959), pp. 136–148.

[64] Georgij Adamovič, "Pamjati Annenskogo," *Cex poètov*, II–III (Berlin: 1922), p. 94.

[65] Varneke, "Annenskij," p. 47.

[66] Fedorov, "Poètičeskoe tvorčestvo Annenskogo," p. 57; Il'in, "Innokentij Annenskij i konec Periklova veka Rossii," p. 51.

[67] D. Blagoj, "Annenskij, Innokentij Fedorovič," *Literaturnaja ènciklopedija*, Vol. I (Moscow: Izdatel'stvo Kommunističeskoj Akademii, 1930. Ann Arbor: American Council of Learned Societies Reprints, Russian Series No. 20, J.W. Edwards, Edwards Bros., Inc., 1948), cols. 165–166.

[68] Geoffrey Brereton, *A Short History of French Literature* (fourth edition. Baltimore: Penguin Books, 1965), pp. 288–290. Like the Parnassians, both Annenskij and Mandel'štam were later to express a renewed interest in the classical world.

[69] Coulter, *Annenskij*, p. 10; Sergej Makovskij, *Portrety sovremennikov* (New York: Chekhov Publishing House, 1955), p. 259. Annenskij translated a number of poems by the Parnassians and Symbolists; these pieces, entitled "parnascy i prokljatye" ("The Parnassians and the Accursed Ones"), were appended to *Tixie pesni*.

[70] Makovskij, *Portrety sovremennikov*, p. 229.

[71] Innokentij Annenskij, "O sovremennom lirizme," *Apollon*, No. 1 (1909), p. 17.

[72] Coulter, *Annenskij*, p. 9. Yet neither in his verse nor in his critical essays was Annenskij a rigid imitator of Mallarmé. Concreteness of images and clarity of expression, posited in his critical writing and practiced in his verse, were a vital component of his aesthetics.

[73] Ginzburg, *O lirike*, p. 346.

[74] Makovskij, *Portrety sovremennikov*, p. 263.

[75] Semen Karlinskij, "Veščestvennost' Annenskogo," *Novyj žurnal*, No. 85 (New York: December, 1966), p. 71; Malnina, "Innokentij Annenskij," p. 213.

[76] Georgij Čulkov, "Zakatnyj zvon (I. Annenskij i Anna Axmatova)," *Otkliki. Literatura. Iskusstvo. Nauka.* (Supplement to newspaper *Den'*), No.

9 (1914), p. 2.

[77]Georgij Čulkov, *Gody stranstvij. Iz knigi vospominanij* (Moscow: Federacija, 1930), p. 190; Blagoj, "Annenskij," col. 166.

[78]Malnina, "Innokentij Annenskij," p. 213; Karlinskij, "Veščestvennost' Annenskogo," p. 71.

[79]Eridano Bazzarelli, *La Poesia di Innokentij Annenskij* (Milan: U. Mursia, 1965), p. 24.

[80]Blagoj, "Annenskij," col. 166; Coulter, *Annenskij*, pp. 9–10.

[81]Fedorov, "Poètičeskoe tvorčestvo Annenskogo," p. 57.

[82]Blagoj, "Annenskij," col. 166.

[83]Coulter, *Annenskij*, p. 27.

[84]Donchin, *French Symbolism*, pp. 107–109. For a discussion of the affinities between Verlaine and Annenskij, see Pozner, *La Littérature Russe*, p. 45.

[85]Setchkarev, *Annenskij*, pp. 16–23.

[86]Valerij Brjusov, *Dalekie i blizkie* (Moscow: Skorpion, 1912), p. 159.

[87]Ginzburg, *O lirike*, p. 331; Sergej Makovskij, "Nikolaj Gumilev po ličnym vospominanijam," *Novyj žurnal*, No. 77 (New York: 1964), p. 163.

CHAPTER TWO

[1]A.S. Bušmin, editor, *Istorija russkoj literatury. Literatura 1890–1917 godov*, Vol. X (Moscow–Leningrad: Akademija Nauk SSSR, 1954), p. 770. Georgette Donchin, *The Influence of French Symbolism on Russian Poetry* ('S-Gravenhage: Mouton and Company, 1958), p. 133.

[2]"Siren' na kamne," *Stixotvorenija i tragedii* (Leningrad: Sovetskij pisatel', 1959), pp. 198–199. Other poems on death are: "Zimnij son," pp. 185–186; "U Sv. Stefana," p. 215; "Pered panixidoj," p. 117; "Serebrjanyj polden'," p. 140; "Umiranie," p. 142; "U groba," p. 66; "Nevozmožno," p. 158; "Aromat lilei mne tjažel," p. 149; "Padenie lilij," pp. 85–86; "Svečka gasnet," p. 82; "Troe," p. 116; "Zimnij poezd," pp. 129–130; "Toska vokzala," p. 128; "Nox vitae," p. 123; and "Černaja vesna," p. 143. For Xodasevič's views on Annenskij's "morbid" inclinations, see Vladislav Xodasevič, "Ob Annenskom," *Èpopeja*, No. 3 (December, 1922), pp. 36–37.

[3]Vsevolod Setchkarev, *Studies in the Life and Work of Innokentij Annenskij* (The Hague: Mouton and Company, 1963), pp. 55, 74.

[4]"Toska," *Stixotvorenija i tragedii*, p. 93. Some of the other important poems in which Annenskij deals with this theme are: "Na poroge," p. 68; "Mučitel'nyj sonet," p. 125; "Želan'e žit'," p. 191; "Tol'ko myslej i slov," pp. 213–214; "Na polotne," p. 194; and "To bylo na Vallen-Koski," pp. 104–105.

[5]For a study of Annenskij's treatment of banality, see Arcadi Nebolsine, *Poshlost* (New York: Columbia University Dissertation, 1971), pp. 112–127.

[6]Donchin, *French Symbolism*, pp. 123–126 ff. Fedorov discusses Annenskij's use of the dream in "Poètičeskoe tvorčestvo Innokentija Annenskogo," *Stixotvorenija i tragedii* (Leningrad: Sovetskij pisatel', 1959), p. 38. For Belyj's view on dreams, see Andrej Belyj, "Na perevale," *Arabeski* (Moscow: 1911. Reprint Munich: Wilhelm Fink Verlag, 1969), p. 242.

[7]Semen Karlinskij, "Veščestvennost' Annenskogo," *Novyj žurnal*, No. 85 (New York: December, 1966), pp. 77–78.

[8]"Dvojnik," *Stixotvorenija i tragedii*, pp. 66–67. Other dream poems include "Träumerei," pp. 107–108 and "Kotoryj?," p. 67.

[9]"Kogda b ne smert', a zabyt'e," *Stixotvorenija i tragedii*, p. 202.

[10]"Utro," *Stixotvorenija i tragedii*, p. 81.

[11]Setchkarev, *Annenskij*, p. 84. See also Catherine Nebolsine Coulter, *Aspects of the Poetry of Innokentij Annenskij* (New York: Columbia University Master's Essay, 1966), pp. 34–35; L. Ja. Ginzburg, *O lirike* (Moscow–Leningrad: Sovetskij pisatel', 1964), p. 334; Aleksandr Buldeev, "I.F. Annenskij kak poèt," *Žatva*, No. 3 (1912), p. 209; E.I. Šamurin, "Osnovnye tečenija v dorevoljucionnoj russkoj poèzii XX veka," in I.S. Ežov and E.I. Šamurin, *Russkaja poèzija XX veka* (Moscow: 1925), p. xxiv.

[12]"Sneg," *Stixotvorenija i tragedii*, pp. 126–127. Other poems about winter are: "Ofort," p. 132; "Ledjanaja tjur'ma," pp. 125–126; and "(Muzyka otdalennoj šarmanki)," pp. 175–176. Irène Agushi feels that snow symbolized beauty to Annenskij. Irène Agushi, *The Poetry of Georgij Ivanov* (Cambridge: Radcliffe College Dissertation, 1960), p. 45. Annenskij associated winter with the crystalline structures of ice and snow, visual symbols of beauty.

[13]"Sneg" first appeared in *Apollon*, No. 1 (1909), p. 16. See A. Fedorov, Notes, in Innokentij Annenskij, *Stixotvorenija i tragedii* (Leningrad: Sovetskij pisatel', 1959), p. 598.

[14]"Poètu," *Stixotvorenija i tragedii*, pp. 219–220. The following lyrics also deal with the poet as an artisan of clear verse: "Drugomu," pp. 156–157; "Zaveščanie," pp. 193–194; and "V volšebnuju prizmu," pp. 115–116. In "V more ljubvi," pp. 224–225, Annenskij parodied some of the excesses of Symbolism.

[15]Setchkarev, *Annenskij*, pp. 38, 70–72; Fedorov, "Poètičeskoe tvorčestvo Annenskogo," p. 37.

[16]The concept of the pre-eminence of form is ultimately derived from Plato. See *The Republic*, translated by Francis MacDonald Cornford (New York: Oxford University Press, 1957), pp. 325, 813 ff.

[17]Setchkarev, *Annenskij*, p. 72. Annenskij posits the art of classical Greece as an aesthetic standard; the classical world figured in the verse of Mandel'štam, although he did not refer to it in his doctrinal essay, "Utro akmeizma."

[18]Clarity and the intrinsic importance of beauty were two important components of the Acmeists' aesthetic values as developed in their doctrinal essays.

[19]Annenskij wrote two lyrics on man as the creator of beauty: "Vesna," *Stixotvorenija i tragedii*, p. 153; and "Osen'," p. 153. Annenskij apparently also thought that the poet should invent a persona of himself as artist. See the sonnet "Čelovek," p. 146. Sergej Makovskij maintains that, although Annenskij told the writers of *Apollon* that they should "invent themselves," he did not follow his own advice. Sergej Makovskij, *Portrety sovremennikov* (New York: Chekhov Publishing House, 1955), p. 241. In "Miraži," Annenskij posits the poet as a reflector. "Miraži," pp. 165–166.

[20]"Bronzovyj poèt," *Stixotvorenija i tragedii*, p. 133. A statue symbolizes the immortality of art in "'Pace,' statuja mira," p. 134. The capacity of art to survive time is the subject of "Ešče lilii," p. 183. Axmatova's treatment of Puškin in Tsarskoe Selo, "Smuglyj otrok brodil po allejam," is the last of a

set of three poems entitled "V Tsarskom Sele," Anna Axmatova, *Sočinenija,* Vol. I (West Germany: Inter–Language Literary Associates, Second Edition, 1967), pp. 63–64.

[21]The further association of the sky with eternity emphasizes the permanence of art.

[22]The usual Russian word for "bronze" being "bronzovyj," the use of this word stresses the link with Puškin's poem.

[23]"Posle koncerta," *Stizotvorenija i tragedii,* p. 138.   The possible impermanence of art is also the theme of "Moj stix," pp. 187–188. Catherine Coulter feels that flowers symbolize the temporary qualities of art for Annenskij.   Coulter, *Annenskij,* p. 61.   This inability to survive, however, is most frequently associated with sound, not visual images.

[24]See also "Siren' na kamne," pp. 198–199 and "Sirenevaja mgla," p. 97.

[25]"Poèzija," p. 65.   For other lyrics in which art is transcendent, see the following: "V aromatnom kraju v ètot den' goluboj," p. 194; "Pervyj fortep'jannyj sonet," pp. 77–78; and "Sredi mirov," p. 165.

[26]The flames of inspiration found in the verse of both Puškin and Annenskij are also related to light, to visual images.

[27]St. Catherine's, an Orthodox monastery, was founded on Mt. Sinai in the sixth century.   Steven Runciman, *The Great Church in Captivity* (Cambridge, England: Cambridge University Press, 1968), p. 133.

[28]Azure was a favorite color associated with Sophia. See Samuel D. Cioran, *Vladimir Solov'ev and the Knighthood of the Divine Sophia* (Waterloo, Canada: Wilfrid Laurier Press, 1977), p. 132.

[29]"Smyčok i struny," *Stizotvorenija i tragedii,* p. 100.   Other poems on this theme are: "Vtoraja fortep'jannyj sonet," p. 92; "Staraja šarmanka," pp. 102–103; "K portretu Dostoevskogo," p. 195; "On i ja," p. 157; "Tretij mučitel'nyj sonet.   strofy," p. 91; "Babočka gaza," p. 167; "Toska pripominanija," p. 120; "Iz zavetnogo fiala," preface to *Tixie pesni,* p. 63; and "Muxi kak mysli," p. 90.

[30]See V.N. Il'in, "Innokentij Annenskij i konec Periklova veka Rossii," *Vozroždenie,* No. 167 (Paris: November, 1965), p. 55.

[31]"Stal'naja cikada," *Stizotvorenija i tragedii,* p. 109.   Other poems about time include: "Lira časov," pp. 181–182; "Toska medlennyx kapel'," p. 161; "OO," pp. 65–66; "Budil'nik," pp. 08–109; and "Toska majatnika," pp. 134–135. "Toska miraža," pp. 210–211, is virtually identical to "Stal'naja cikada."

[32]"Nocturno," *Stizotvorenija i tragedii,* p. 175.   See also: "V nebe li merknet zvezda," pp. 201–202; "Bessonnica rebenka," p. 83; "Mig," p. 193; "Minuta," pp. 212–213; and "Janvarskaja skazka," p. 111.

[33]Sergej Makovskij thought that art represented an escape from death (i.e., time) for Annenskij. Makovskij, *Portrety sovremennikov,* p. 243.

CHAPTER THREE

[1]Vsevolod Setchkarev, *Studies in the Life and Work of Innokentij Annenskij* (The Hague: Mouton and Company, 1963), p. 129.

[2]Catherine Nebolsine Coulter, *Aspects of the Poetry of Innokentij Annenskij* (New York: Columbia University Master's Essay, 1966), p. 36.

[3]"Toska vozvrata," Innokentij Annenskij, *Stixotvorenija i tragedii* (Leningrad: Sovetskij pisatel', 1959), p. 87.

[4]"Pered panixidoj," *Stixotvorenija i tragedii*, p. 117.

[5]"Moja Toska," *Stixotvorenija i tragedii*, pp. 171-172. Personification of an abstraction as a woman can also be seen in the following: "Poèzija," p. 65; "Sredi mirov," p. 165; and "Na poroge (Trinadcat' strok)," p. 68. Conscience ("Sovest'," a feminine noun) is personified in "K portretu Dostoevskogo," *Stixotvorenija i tragedii*, p. 195, Annenskij stressing the vital role of conscience as the shaper of Dostoevskij's values, the force making him at once a prophet (philosopher and seer) and artist (novelist).

[6]"Maki," *Stixotvorenija i tragedii*, p. 99.

[7]"Probuždenie," *Stixotvorenija i tragedii*, pp. 116-117. Nature is personified also in the following: "Vesna," p. 153; "Drugomu," pp. 156-157; "Svečka gasnet," p. 82; and "Neživaja," pp. 131-132.

[8]"Staraja šarmanka," *Stixotvorenija i tragedii*, pp. 102-103. An instrument is personified in "Smyčok i struny" as well. "Smyčok i struny," p. 100.

[9]"Vtoroj fortep'jannyj sonet," *Stixotvorenija i tragedii*, p. 92. The personification of art can also be seen in "'Pace,' statuja mira," p. 134 and "Bronzovyj poèt," p. 133.

[10]Annenskij's equation of music with sculpture exemplifies his vision of art as concrete and three-dimensional.

[11]Wasps also figure in the verse of Mandel'štam. See K. Taranovskij, "Pčely i osy v poèzii Mandel'štama: k voprosu o vlijanii Vjačeslava Ivanova na Mandel'štama," in the collection *To Honor Roman Jakobson. Essays on the Occasion of his 70th Birthday* (The Hague: Mouton and Company, 1967), pp. 1973-1995.

[12]"Veter," *Stixotvorenija i tragedii*, p. 73. Annenskij personified wind or storm in the following as well: "Toska otšumevšej grozy," p. 119; "Decrescendo," p. 200; "Pod novoj kryšej," pp. 75-76; and "Nebo zvezdami v tumane . . .," p. 154.

[13]"Oktjabr'skij mif," *Stixotvorenija i tragedii*, p. 122. Fog, snow, and other forms of moisture (including bodies of water) are personified in the following: "Sirenevaja mgla," p. 97; "Sneg," pp. 126-127; "Serebrjannyj polden'," p. 140; "Vesennij romans," p. 164; and "V aromatnom kraju v ètot den' goluboj," p. 194.

[14]"Za ogradoj," *Stixotvorenija i tragedii*, pp. 200-201. The sun and moon are personified in these lyrics also: "Mesjac," pp. 160-161; "Dekoracija," p. 82; and "Paralleli," pp. 92-93.

[15]"Listy," *Stixotvorenija i tragedii*, p. 68. For further personification of nature, see the following: "Dremotnost'," pp. 162-163; "Dymnye tuči," p. 192; "Avgust. 2. Električeskij svet v allee," p. 72; "Želan'e žit'," p. 191; "V marte," pp. 100-101; and "Verbnaja nedelja," p. 103.

[16]"Zimnij poezd," *Stixotvorenija j tragedii*, pp. 129-130. The personification of death also figures in "Černaja vesna," p. 143; "Prizraki," pp. 143-144; and "U Sv. Stefana," p. 215.

[17]"Ty opjat' so mnoj," *Stixotvorenija i tragedii*, pp. 103-104.

[18]"Toska sada," *Stixotvorenija i tragedii*, p. 192.

[19]This has been noted by a number of critics, including: Semen Karlinskij, "Veščestvennost' Annenskogo," *Novyj žurnal*, No. 85 (New York: December, 1966), pp. 73-74; Vladimír Pozner, *Moderní Ruská Literatura. 1885-1932*

(Prague: Jan Laichter Publishers, 1932), p. 19; A. Evgen'ev, "Stixotvorenija Innokentija Annenskogo," *Literaturnoe obozrenie*, No. 14 (1939), p. 31; L. Ja. Ginzburg, *O lirike* (Moscow–Leningrad: Sovetskij pisatel', 1964), pp. 346–347. There has also been some discussion of a related phenomenon, his use of prosaisms in verse. The use of prosaisms, employed later by Axmatova, demonstrates Annenskij's proximity to the prose of the early twentieth century. For an examination of this, see the following: Johannes Holthusen, *Russische Gegenwartsliteratur. I. 1890–1940. Die literarische Avantgarde* (Bern and Munich: Francke Verlag, 1963), p. 50; Viktor Gofman, "Innokentij Annenskij, 'Kiparisovyj larec,'" *Novyj žurnal dlja vsex*, No. 21 (June, 1910), col. 122; Aleksandr Buldeev, "I.F. Annenskij kak poèt," *Žatva*, No. 3 (1912), pp. 195–196; L. Ja. Ginzburg, "O prozaizmax v lirike Bloka," *Blokovskij sbornik* (Tartu: Tartuskij gosudarstvennyj universitet, 1964), pp. 158, 161; Lubov Alex Shapovaloff, *The Aesthetics and Poetics of Innokentij Annenskij* (Seattle: University of Washington Dissertation, 1968), pp. 341–342; and Coulter, *Annenskij*, p. 23.

[20] "U groba," *Stixotvorenija i tragedii*, p. 66.

[21] "Zaveščanie," *Stixotvorenija i tragedii*, pp. 193–194.

[22] "Poslednie sireni," *Stixotvorenija i tragedii*, pp. 215–216. Annenskij often equates the withering of flowers with death, here with the death of affection. Other lyrics with concretizations involving nature include "To i èto," pp. 113–114; and "Starye èstonki," pp. 216–218.

[23] "Zabvenie," *Stixotvorenija i tragedii*, pp. 159–160. Analogous similes are contained in: "Ofort," p. 132, "Zakatnyj zvon v pole," p. 147; "Kulačiška," pp. 114–115; "Tretij mučitel'nyj sonet. strofy," p. 91; "Konec osennej skazki," p. 80; and "Preljudija," p. 138.

[24] "V volšebnuju prizmu," *Stixotvorenija i tragedii*, pp. 115–116. Annenskij uses similar metaphors in the following: "Kievskie peščery," p. 113; "Aromat lilej mne tjažel," p. 149; "Siren' na kamne," pp. 198–199; "Ešče lilii," p. 183; "Černoe more," p. 189; and "Pered zakatom," p. 75.

[25] "Maj," *Stixotvorenija i tragedii*, pp. 69–70. For other concretizing metaphors involving nature, see the following: "Doždik," pp. 121–122; "Bronzovyj poèt," p. 133; "Pervyj fortep'jannyj sonet," pp. 77–78; "Opjat' v doroge," pp. 178–179; "(Muzyka otdalennoj šarmanki)," pp. 175–176; "Umiranie," p. 142; "Toska mimoletnosti," p. 98; "Ametisty," p. 110; "Kogda b ne smert', a zabyt'e," p. 202; "Kartinka," pp. 136–137; "Osen'," pp. 147–148; "Majskaja groza," pp. 195–196; and "Toska sinevy," p. 191.

[26] Catherine Coulter has observed that this device was also employed by Fet. Coulter, *Annenskij*, p. 14.

[27] "Toska miraža," *Stixotvorenija i tragedii*, pp. 210–211.

[28] "Oktjabr'skij mif," *Stixotvorenija i tragedii*, p. 122.

[29] "Zaveščanie," *Stixotvorenija i tragedii*, pp. 193–194.

[30] "Za ogradoj," *Stixotvorenija i tragedii*, pp. 200–201.

[31] This is true of Axmatova's verse as well.

CHAPTER FOUR

[1] Annenskij's critical abilities have been attested to by several scholars. Lev Vojtolovskij felt that Annenskij was a critic with original ideas. Lev

Vojtolovskij, "Innokentij Annenskij," *Očerki istorii russkoj literatury XIX i XX vekov. čast' vtoraja, Rešetnikov-Gor'kij* (Moscow–Leningrad: State Publishing House, 1928), p. 233. Jur'eva described him as a sensitive critic. Zoja Jur'eva, "Innokentij Annenskij o Gogole," *Novyj žurnal*, No. 45 (New York: June, 1956), p. 139. Sergej Makovskij asserted, however, that Annenskij's criticism was subjective, serving him as a form of aesthetic confession. Sergej Makovskij, *Na Parnase serebrjanogo veka* (Munich: Verlag ZOPE, 1962), pp. 127–128 ff.

[2]Innokentij Annenskij, *Kniga otraženij* (St. Petersburg: Bašmačnikov Brothers, 1906. Reprint Munich: Wilhelm Fink Verlag, 1969); *Vtoraja kniga otraženij* (St. Petersburg: Bašmačnikov Brothers, 1909. Reprint Munich: Wilhelm Fink Verlag, 1969).

[3]D.S. Mirsky, *A History of Russian Literature. II. After 1881*, edited and abridged by Francis J. Whitfield (New York: Alfred A. Knopf, 1949), p. 447; L. [jubov'] G. [urevič], "Pamjati I.F. Annenskogo," *Russkaja mysl'*, No. 1, Pt. II (1910), p. 165.

[4]Gurevič, "Pamjati I.F. Annenskogo," p. 164. Varneke considered Annenskij's essays "whimsical, refined, unusual, and accidental." B. Varneke, "I.F. Annenskij" [Nekrolog], *Žurnal Ministerstva narodnogo prosveščenija*, No. 3 (1910), p. 45. According to Kornej Čukovskij, *Kniga otraženij* was a "notebook of impressions" that did not prove anything but rather argued with everything and polemicized with everyone. Kornej Čukovskij, "Ob èstetičeskom nigilizme," *Vesy*, Nos. 3–4 (1906), p. 79.

[5]A. Fedorov, "Poètičeskoe tvorčestvo Innokentija Annenskogo," Innokentij Annenskij, *Stixotvorenija i tragedii* (Leningrad: Sovetskij pisatel', 1959), p. 15.

[6]*Apollon* would eventually be the mouthpiece of the Acmeists.

[7]"O sovremennom lirizme," 'Oni,' Pt. 1, *Apollon*, No. 1 (October, 1909), pp. 12–42; 'Oni,' Pt. 2, *Apollon*, No. 2 (November, 1909), pp. 3–29; 'One,' *Apollon*, No. 3 (December, 1909), pp. 5–29. The projected essay 'Ono' was never written. Lubov Alex Shapovaloff, *The Aesthetics and Poetics of Innokentij Annenskij* (Seattle: University of Washington Dissertation, 1968), pp. 50–51.

[8]Denis Mickiewicz, "*Apollo* and Modernist Poetics," *Russian Literature Triquarterly* (Fall, 1971), pp. 234–235.

[9]Ljubov' Guręvič, *Literatura i èstetika* (Moscow: Russkaja mysl', 1912), p. 100. Georgij Čulkov was critical of "O sovremennom lirizme." Georgij Čulkov, *Gody stranstvij. Iz knigi vospominanij* (Moscow: Federacija, 1930), p. 191.

[10]This divergence, noted in Chapter One, will be discussed again in the concluding chapter.

[11]"Stixotvorenija Ja. P. Polonskogo kak pedagogičeskij material," *Vospitanie i obučenie*, No. 5 (May, 1887), pp. 109–118; No. 6 (June, 1887), pp. 133–142; "Sočinenija gr. A.K. Tolstogo kak pedagogičeskij material," *Vospitanie i obučenie*, No. 8 (August, 1887), pp. 181–191. Annenskij was also a well known classical scholar who translated a number of Euripides' plays. *Teatr Evripida* (St. Petersburg: 1907; 2nd edition Vols. I–III, Moscow: 1916–1921). He did not strive for accuracy in his translations, for he modernized the language of the original and added many observations in the margins; his renditions were modern versions of Euripides. B. Varneke, "Teatr Evripida," *Žurnal Ministerstva narodnogo prosveščenija*, No. 5 (1907), pp. 226, 228. His work in Greek drama includes the essay "Antičnaja tragedija" ("Ancient Tragedy"), which was delivered as a public lecture in St. Petersburg in 1902 prior to its publication in *Mir Božij* (November, 1902), pp. 1–41.

[12] "Problema Gogolevskogo jumora," *Kniga otraženij*, pp. 1–27; "Èstetika 'Mertvyx duš' i ee nasled'e," *Apollon*, No. 8 (1911), pp. 50–58.

[13] "Dostoevskij do katastrofy," *Kniga otraženij*, pp. 29–57; "Drama nastroenija," *Ibid.*, pp. 147–167; "Umirajuščij Turgenev," *Ibid.*, pp. 59–73.

[14] Annenskij mentioned the French Symbolists only in passing, however. Innokentij Annenskij, "Antičnyj mif v sovremennoj francuzskoj poèzii," *Germes*, No. 7 (1908), pp. 177–185; No. 8 (1908), pp. 209–213; No. 9 (1908), pp. 236–240; and No. 10 (1908), pp. 270–288. He considered the Parnassian poet Hérédia and the Belgian Symbolist Verhaeren as having been very influential, stating also that Baudelaire was the "first poet of the *contemporary*" city and that Verlaine, Rimbaud, Tristan Corbière and others were extremely important also. "O sovremennom lirizme," 'Oni,' Pt. 2, pp. 4, 29.

[15] "Bal'mont lirik," *Kniga otraženij*, pp. 169–213. Kornej Čukovskij considered this the best study on Bal'mont, and Varneke and Makovskij also thought highly of it. Kornej Čukovskij, "Innokentij Annenskij," *Reč'*, No. 336 (7 December, 1909), p. 4; Varneke, "Annenskij," p. 44; Sergej Makovskij, *Portrety sovremennikov* (New York: Chekhov Publishing House, 1955), p. 254.

[16] "O sovremennom lirizme," 'Oni,' Pt. 2, p. 29.

[17] "O sovremennom lirizme," 'Oni,' Pt. 1, p. 12–13.

[18] *Ibid.*, pp. 22.

[19] "O sovremennom lirizme," 'Oni,' Pt. 2, p. 13.

[20] "O sovremennom lirizme," 'Oni,' Pt. 1, p. 23.

[21] *Ibid.*, pp. 25–27 ff.

[22] Annenskij noted an exotic strain in Gumilev's poetry, relating this to the younger poet's love for the "refined and strange." He praised Gumilev for unerring taste in the choice of poetic scenery. *Ibid.*, p. 25. "O sovremennom lirizme," 'Oni,' Pt. 2, p. 25.

[23] G.P. Struve, publication and commentary, "Innokentij Annenskij i Gumilev. 'Neizvestnaja' stat'ja Annenskogo," *Novyj žurnal*, No. 78 (New York: 1964), p. 284.

[24] *Ibid.*, pp. 286–287. Nikolaj Ocup recalls in his memoirs that Annenskij regarded the verse of the gymnasium student Gorenko (Axmatova) very highly, preferring it to the lyrics of Gumilev. Nikolaj Ocup, *Sovremenniki* (Paris: Imprimerie Cooperative Étoile, 1961), p. 25.

[25] Innokentij Annenskij, "Ob èstetičeskom otnošenii Lermontova k prirode," *Russkaja škola*, No. 12 (December, 1891), p. 74; "Bal'mont lirik," pp. 177–181. Annenskij also felt that a social role should not be inflicted on poetry. "Ob èstetičeskom otnošenii Lermontova k prirode." pp. 74–75.

[26] "Tragičeskaja Medeja," Pt. 3, *Žurnal Ministerstva narodnogo prosveščesnija*, No. 11 (1903), p. 500.

[27] "Stixotvorenija Ja. P. Polonskogo," p. 134.

[28] Annenskij felt that the sensation of beauty in poetry was often closely linked with an awareness of nature. The "aesthetic attitude toward nature was not at all primordial," he stated, but "was developed with other spiritual characteristics of man." "Ob Èstetičeskom otnošenii Lermontova k prirode," p. 75.

[29] "Simvoly krasoty u russkix pisatelej," *Vtoraja kniga otraženij*, p. 12.

[30] *Ibid.*, pp. 10–11.

[31] Annenskij's separation here of suffering and artistic creation seems to contradict the aesthetic views put forth in "The Bow and Strings" and "The Barrel Organ," but in these lyrics, he links that torment with sound, specifically, with music, not with the visual arts.

[32] "Iz nabljudenij nad jazykom russkogo Severa," *Sbornik v čest' V.I. Lamanskogo* (St. Petersburg: 1883), pp. 196–211. Varneke referred to this article in his obituary on Annenskij. Varneke, "Annenskij," p. 38.

[33] "Čto takoe poèzija." Posthumous article, *Apollon*, No. 6 (1911), p. 52.

[34] "Pedagogičeskie pis'ma. tret'e pis'mo," *Russkaja škola*, No. 2 (1895), p. 98. Annenskij also stressed the intrinsic value of the word in "Bal'mont lirik," p. 172.

[35] "Pedagogičeskie pis'ma. pervoe pis'mo. Jazyki v srednej škole," *Russkaja škola*, Nos. 7–8 (1892), p. 165. In his study of Polonskij, Annenskij noted the link between the poet and his cultural heritage. "Stixotvorenija Ja. P. Polonskogo," p. 134. He further stated that the spoken language was closer to poetry than to prose. *Ibid.*, p. 134.

[36] "Bal'mont lirik," pp. 172–173.

[37] *Ibid.*, p. 171.

[38] "Xudožestvennyj idealizm Gogolja," p. 116.

[39] "Stixotvorenija Ja. P. Polonskogo," pp. 134, 139.

[40] "Ob èstetičeskom otnošenii Lermontova k prirode," p. 74.

[41] "Bal'mont lirik," p. 202.

[42] "Ob èstetičeskom otnošenii Lermontova k prirode," p. 75. The poet, said Annenskij, "seeks to impart to his symbols not only a general exposure of life in its contours and colors, but . . . life itself." "Xudožestvennyj idealizm Gogolja," p. 116. Annenskij's inclusion of the symbol within the confines of the physical world strips this device of the extra–literary significance it had acquired under Russian Symbolism.

CHAPTER FIVE

[1] Viktor Žirmunskij, "Preodolevšie simvolizm," *Russkaja mysl'*, No. 12 (1916), p. 30; A. A. Volkov, *Russkaja literatura XX veka. dooktjabr'skij period* (Moscow: Prosveščenie, 1964), p. 400. Volkov notes that the earliest stirrings of Acmeism were made public in the small journal *Giperborej* (1912), and in several publications of "Cex poètov," as well as in the manifestoes of 1913.

[2] Vladimir Pozner, *Panorama de la Littérature Russe Contemporaine* (Paris: Kra, 1929), p. 225.

[3] E. Aničkov, *Novaja russkaja poèzija* (Berlin: I. P. Ladyžnikov, 1922. Reprint The Hague: Mouton and Company, 1969), pp. 111–112.

[4] Marie Maline, *Nicolas Gumilev: Poète et critique acméiste* (Brussels: Palais des Académies, 1964), p. 20. For a more detailed account of the Guild of Poets, consult the following: Jeanne Rude, *Anna Akhmatova* (Paris: Éditions Seghers, 1968), p. 65; Leonid Strakhovsky, *Craftsmen of the Word: Three Poets of Modern Russia* (Cambridge: Harvard University Press, 1949. 2nd edition Westbridge, Connecticut: Greenwood Press, 1969), pp. 23–27; Howard William Chalsma, *Russian Acmeism: Its History, Doctrine, and Poetry* (Seattle: University of Washington Dissertation, 1967), p. 47. Vladimir Pjast

[Pestovskij], *Vstreči* (Moscow: Federacija,   1929),   p.   208;   Gleb Struve,
"Tvorčeskij put' Gumileva," in N. Gumilev, *Sobranie sočinenij v četyrex tomax,*
edited by G. P.   Struve and B. A. Filippov, Vol II (Washington, D.C.:
Viktor Kamkin, Inc., 1964), p. x; Sergej Makovskij, *Na Parnase serebrjanogo
veka* (Munich: Verlag ZOPE, 1962), p. 220; Anna Gumileva, "Nikolaj
Stepanovič Gumilev," *Novyj žurnal,* No. 46 (New York: 1956), p. 117.
Axmatova noted that the Guild discussed the program for Acmeism in a
meeting   at   Tsarskoe   Selo.   Anna   Axmatova,   "Mandel'štam   (listki   iz
dnevnika)," in Anna Axmatova, *Sočinenija,* edited by G. P.   Struve and B. A.
Filippov, Vol. II (New York: Inter–Language Literary Associates, 1968), pp.
173–174.

[5]Strakhovsky, *Craftsmen,* p. 29; Maline, *Gumilev,* pp.   21, 64; Chalsma,
Acmeism, p. 53.

[6]Gleb Struve, "N. S. Gumilev. Žizn' i ličnost'," in N. Gumilev, *Sobranie
sočinenij v četyrex tomax,* edited by G. P. Struve and B. A. Filippov, Vol. I
(Washington, D.C.: Viktor Kamkin, Inc., 1962), pp. ix, xl.

[7]They include: *Put' konkvistadorov* (1905), *Romantičeskie cvety* (first
edition, 1908), *Žemčuga* (first edition, 1910), *Čužoe nebo* (1912), *Kolčan* (1916),
Koster (1918), and *Šater* (first edition, 1921).   The collection *Ognennyj stolp*
was published after his death in 1921.   See Earl Delos Sampson, *Studies in the
Poetic   Technique   of   Nikolaj   Gumilev* (Cambridge: Harvard   University
Dissertation,   1968),   p.   11.   A   posthumous   collection,   *Stixotvorenija.*
Posmertnyj sbornik, came out in 1922, and the collection *K sinej zvezde* was
published in 1923.   *Ibid.,* pp. 11–12.

[8]Maline, *Gumilev,* pp. 63–64.   "Zavety simvolizma i akmeizm" came out
in *Apollon,* No. 1, 1913.   When it was reprinted in N. S. Gumilev, *Pis'ma o
russkoj poèzii* (Petrograd: Mysl', 1923), pp. 37–42, the word "zavety" had
been changed to "nasledie" ("legacy").   Gleb Struve, "Notes," in N. Gumilev,
Sobranie   sočinenij   v   četyrex   tomax,   edited   by   G.   P.   Struve   and   B.   A.
Filippov, Vol. IV (Washington, D.C.:   Victor Kamkin, Inc., 1968), p.   599.
"Žizn' stixa" was also reprinted in *Pis'ma o russkoj poèzii* and contained a
discussion of Symbolism, as well as assertions that art was intended to be
only art and that poetry was a living organism.

[9]I. S. Ežov and E. I. Šamurin, *Russkaja poèzija XX veka* (Moscow:
1925), p. 570.   N. E. Krutikova and I.   T. Kruk, *Russkaja literatura XX veka.
dooktjabr'skij period* (Kiev: Višča škola, 1970), p. 274; and I. V. Vladislavslev
[Ignatij Vladislavlevič Gul'binskij], *Russkie pisateli XIX–XX st.* (Moscow:
Nauka, 1913), p. 124.

[10]Sam Driver, "Acmeism," *The Slavic and East European Journal,* Vol.
XII, No. 2 (1968), p. 156, note 2.

[11]Jurij Terapiano, "Osip Mandel'štam," *Grani,* No. 50 (Frankfurt: 1961),
pp. 109–110.

[12]Gleb Struve, "O. È. Mandel'štam.   Opyt biografii i kritičeskogo
kommentarija," in Osip Mandel'štam, *Sobranie sočinenij v trex tomax,* edited
by G. P. Struve and B.   A. Filippov, Vol. I (2nd edition Washington, D.C.:
Inter–Language Literary Associates, 1967), pp. xxx, lxxi–lxxiii.   Although there
has been some controversy concerning the date of his death,   Nadežda
Mandel'štam has confirmed that the death certificate she received gave 27
December, 1938 as the death date.   The article in the *Kratkaja literaturnaja
ènciklopedija* concurs.   Nadežda Mandel'štam, *Vospominanija* (New York:
Chekhov Publishing House, 1970), p. 395; Al. Morozov, "Mandel'štam, Osip
Èmil'evič," *Kratkaja literaturnaja ènciklopedija,* Vol.   IV (Moscow: Sovetskaja
ènciklopedija, 1967), col. 568.

[13]Strakhovsky, *Craftsmen*, p. 86; Glev Struve, "Mandel'štam," p. xxxix.
Tristia appeared in Berlin in 1922, while a third collection, *Vtoraja kniga*,
came out in 1923. Ežov i Šamurin, *Russkaja poèzija XX veka*, p. 578.
Another collection, *Stixotvorenija*, was published in 1928.

[14]His prose works *Šum vremeni* (including *Feodosia*) and *Egipetskaja
marka* appeared in 1925 and 1928, respectively. Gleb Struve and B. A.
Filippov, Bibliography, in Osip Mandel'štam, *Sobranie sočinenij v trex tomax*,
edited by G. P. Struve and B. A. Filippov, Vol. III (New York:
Inter-Language Literary Associates, 1969), p. 426. In recognition of
Mandel'štam's critical gifts, a translation of his essays and letters has recently
been published. Mandelstam, *The Complete Critical Prose and Letters*, edited
by Jane Gary Harris, translated by Jane Gary Harris and Constance Link
(Ann Arbor: Ardis, 1979).

[15]"Utro akmeizma" was not published until 1919. Struve, "Mandel'štam,"
p. xxxviii. In "O sobesednike," Mandel'štam discussed the Symbolist poet and
sound. He focused on Bal'mont, on the role of the poet as interlocutor, and
on Acmeism and the word. Gleb Struve and B.A. Filippov, Notes, in Osip
Mandel'štam, *Sobranie sočinenij v dvux tomax*, edited by G.P. Struve and B.A.
Filippov, Vol. II (New York: Inter-Language Literary Associates, 1966), p.
589. "Slovo i kul'tura" was first published in the miscellany of Cex poètov,
Drakon, in 1921. Here Mandel'štam treated the function of the word in
poetry and classicism. In "O prirode slova," first published as a separate
brochure in Xar'kov in 1922, he dealt with Acmeism, touching once again on
the word. He also reacted negatively to Andrej Belyj. "Burja i natisk"
appeared in *Russkoe iskusstvo*, No. 1 (1923); Mandel'štam discussed
Symbolism and Futurism in this essay and touched also on Annenskij,
speaking very highly of his abilities and noting the considerable influence he
had had upon later poets.

Boris Bukhshtab felt that Mandel'štam was profoundly alien to Acmeism
in that he struggled against the simple "correspondence" of the word to the
thing it signifies—something for which the Acmeists were striving. In "Slovo
i kul'tura," said Bukhshtab, Mandel'štam wanted to free the word from
designating an object. Boris Bukhshtab, "The Poetry of Mandelstam,"
Russian Literature Triquarterly (Fall, 1971), p. 271. What Mandel'štam may
in fact have been doing was establishing the significance of the existence of
the word (the importance of the word as an object in its right). See the
discussion of "Utro akmeizma" later in this chapter.

[16]For discussions of Axmatova as a lyricist, see the following: Gleb
Struve, "Anna Akhmatova," in Anna Axmatova, *Sočinenija*, edited by G. P.
Struve and B. A. Filippov, Vol. I (2nd edition New York: Inter-Language
Literary Associates, 1967), p. 14; A. Selivanovskij, "Očerki russkoj poèzii XX
veka. glava vtoraja. Raspad akmeizma," *Literaturnaja učeba*, No. 8 (1934),
pp. 25, 29; Julij Ajxenval'd, *Siluèty russkix pisatelej* (Berlin: Slovo, 1923.
Reprint The Hague: Mouton and Company, 1969), p. 280; Sam Driver,
"Anna Akhmatova: Early Love Poems," *Russian Literature Triquarterly* (Fall,
1971), p. 306; Kornej Čukovskij, "Axmatova i Majakovskij," *Dom Iskusstv*, No.
1 (1921), p. 27; Žirmunskij, "Preodolevšie simvolizm," p. 34; Boris
Éjxenbaum, *Anna Axmatova. opyt analiza* (Petrograd: Petropečat', 1923), pp.
104–105; E. S. Dobin, *Poèzija Anny Axmatovoj* (Leningrad: Sovetskij pisatel',
1968), pp. 77–78.

[17]Gleb Struve, "Akhmatova," p. 6. For Axmatova's birth and death
dates, see Struve, "Akhmatova," p. 5. Her first poems, signed with the
initials "A. G.," appeared in the Paris journal *Sirius* in 1907. Rude,
Akhmatova, pp. 13–14. Her verse collections include *Večer* (1912), *Četki*
(1913), *Podorožnik* (1921), the *poèma U samogo morja* (1921), and *Anno
Domini MCMXXI* (1921). Ežov and Šamurin, *Russkaja poèzija XX veka*, p.

562. Her verse output also includes *Belaja staja* (1917), *Iz šesti knig* (1940), *Rekviem* (written 1940, published in Munich in 1963), and the *Poèma bez geroja* (written 1940-1962). Rude, *Akhmatova*, pop. 85-86; G. P. Struve and B. A. Filippov, Bibliography, Anna Axmatova, *Sočinenija*, edited by G. P. Struve and B. A. Filippov, Vol. II (New York: Inter-Language Literary Associates, 1968), pp. 95-132.

[18] Geoffrey Brereton, *A Short History of French Literature* (4th edition. Baltimore: Penguin Books, 1965), p. 288; Andrej Levinson, "Gumilev," *Sovremennye zapiski*, No. 9 (Paris, 1922), p. 312; Aničkov, *Novaja russkaja poèzija*, p. 109.

[19] Gumilev objected to the Parnassian tendency to regard the word as a mere object. Renato Poggioli, *The Poets of Russia, 1890-1930* (Cambridge: Harvard University Press, 1960), p. 227.

[20] Gumilev's love of adventure is yet another link between him and the Parnassians, particularly Hérédia. A. Fedorov, "Poètičeskoe tvorčestvo Innokentija Annenskogo," Innokentij Annenskij, *Stixotvorenija i tragedii* (Leningrad: Sovetskij pisatel', 1959), p. 56; Driver, "Acmeism," p. 151.

[21] Jurij Verxovskij, "Put' poèta. O poèzii N. S. Gumileva," *Sovremennaja literatura* (Leningrad: Mysl', 1925), p. 114.

[22] Brereton, *French Literature*, p. 289; Fedorov, "Poètičeskoe tvorčestvo Annenskogo," p. 57.

[23] Rude, *Akhmatova*, p. 64; Verxovskij, "O poèzii Gumileva," pp. 124-125.

[24] E. I. Šamurin, "Osnovnye tečenija v dorevoljucionnoj russkoj poèzii XX veka," in I. S. Ežov and E. I. Šamurin, *Russkaja poèzija XX veka* (Moscow: 1925), p. xxvi; Maline, *Gumilev*, p. 21.

[25] Victor Erlich, *Russian Formalism. History-Doctrine* (2nd edition The Hague: Mouton and Company, 1965), pp. 41-42. Selivanovskij also noted a connection between Symbolism and Acmeism. Aleksej Selivanovskij, *Očerki po istorii russkoj sovetskoj poèzii* (Moscow: Xudožestvennaja literatura, 1936), p. 48.

[26] Chalsma, *Russian Acmeism*, p. 63. The following critics considered Acmeism a continuation of Symbolism: A. Dolinin, "Akmeizm," *Zavety*, No. 5, Pt. 2 (May, 1913), p. 160; Valerij Brjusov, "Novye tečenija v russkoj poèzii. Akmeizm," *Russkaja mysl'*, No. 4 (1913), p. 135; Valerij Brjusov, "Iskusstvo i literatura RSFSR v èpoxu revoljucii (1917-1922). Včera, segodnja i zavtra russkoj poèzii," *Pečat' i revoljucija*, No. 7 (July, 1922), p. 51; Sergej Bobrov, "Osip Mandel'štam. *Tristia*," *Pečat' i revoljucija*, No. 4 (April, 1923), pp. 259-260; D. S. Mirsky, *Modern Russian Literature* (London: Oxford University Press, 1925), p. 109; Selivanovskij, *Očerki po istorii russkoj sovetskoj poèzii*, p. 49; Sergej Makovskij, *Portrety sovremennikov* (New York: Chekhov Publishing House, 1955), pp. 386-387; Vladimir Markov, "Mysli o russkom futurizme," *Novyj žurnal*, No. 38 (New York: 1954), p. 172. Markov is extremely negative toward Acmeism, blaming it for the philistinism of Soviet literature. The Acmeists were, however, hostile to Soviet politics, were drawn to Western cultural achievements, and were intensely private lyricists.

[27] Anič'kov, *Novaja russkaja poèzija*, p. 109.

[28] Clarence Brown, "The Prose of Osip Mandelstam (introductory essay)," Clarence Brown, *The Prose of Osip Mandelstam* (Princeton: Princeton University Press, 1965), p. 13.

[29] Boris Èjxenbaum, *Anna Axmatova. opyt analiza* (Petrograd: Petropečat', 1923), p. 24.

[30] Žirmunskij, "Preodolevšie simvolizm," p. 28. He expressed a similar

view in *Voprosy teorii literatury (stat'i 1916-1926)* (Leningrad: 1928. Reprint 'S-Gravenhage: Mouton and Company, 1962), p. 183.

[31]V. Sajanov, *Ot klassikov k sovremennosti. Kritičeskie stat'i* (Leningrad: Priboj, 1929), p. 106.

[32]Gleb Struve, "Tvorčeskij put' Gumileva," p. xvi.

[33]Acmeism has been termed a rebellion against Romanticism, a return to classicism, particularly in regard to Axmatova. Žirmunskij, *Voprosy teorii literatury*, p. 189; Aničkov, *Novaja russkaja poèzija*, p. 64; Gleb Struve, "Tri sud'by (Blok, Gumilev, Sologub)," *Novyj žurnal*, No. 17 (New York: 1947), p. 197; Helen Muchnic, "Three Inner Emigrés: Anna Akhmatova, Osip Mandelshtam, Nikolai Zabolotsky," *The Russian Review*, Vol. 26 (January, 1967), pp. 14-15. For Žirmunskij's thoughts on this subject, see Samurin, "Osnovnye tečenija," p. xxii.

[34]Žirmunskij, "Preodolevšie simvolizm," pp. 29-30, 55; L. Ja. Ginzburg, *O lirike* (Moscow-Leningrad: Sovetskij pisatel', 1964), pp. 363-364; Selivanovskij, *Očerki po istorii russkoj sovetskoj poèzii*, pp. 49, 51; Makovskij, *Na Parnase serebrjanogo veka*, p. 220; Strakhovsky, *Craftsmen*, p. 10; Georgij Adamovič, "Kommentarii," *Cex poètov*, No. 4 (Berlin: 1923), p. 62; Krystyna Pomorska, *Russian Formalist Theory and its Poetic Ambiance* (The Hague: Mouton and Company, 1968), p. 51.

[35]Gleb Struve, "Pis'ma o russkoj poèzii," *Russkaja mysl'*, Nos. 6-7 (Prague: 1922), p. 240; Žirmunskij, *Voprosy teorii literatury*, p. 189.

[36]Erlich, *Russian Formalism*, p. 41; Selivanovskij, *Očerki po istorii russkoj sovetskoj poèzii*, p. 50; Alexander Kaun, "Russian Poetic Trends on the Eve of and the Morning After 1917," *The Slavic Year Book* (American Series, I), Being Vol. XX of *The Slavonic and East European Review* (1941), p. 59.

[37]Žirmunskij, "Preodolevšie simvolizm," p. 31; Pozner, *La Littérature Russe*, p. 226.

[38]This was especially true of Axmatova. K.[onstantin] Močul'skij, "Poètičeskoe tvorčestvo Anny Axmatovoj," *Russkaja mysl'*, Nos. 3-4 (Sofia: 1921), p. 185; Valer'jan Poljanskij, "Social'nye korni russkoj poèzii ot simvolistov do našix dnej," in I. S. Ežov and E. I. Samurin, *Russkaja poèzija XX veka* (Moscow: 1925), p. xiii; Driver, "Acmeism," p. 151.

[39]Struve, "Pis'ma o russkoj poèzii," p. 240; Močul'skij, "Poètičeskoe tvorčestvo Anny Axmatovoj," p. 201; Žirmunskij, "Preodolevšie simvolizm," p. 30.

[40]Selivanovskij, *Očerki po istorii russkoj sovetskoj poèzii*, pp. 49-50.

[41]Žirmunskij, "Preodolevšie simvolizm," p. 29; Vasilij L'vov-Rogačevskij, *Novejšaja russkaja literatura* (3rd edition Moscow-Leningrad: L. D. Frenkel', 1924), p. 286. For a discussion of the linearity that informed art in St. Petersburg, see Beverly Whitney Kean, *All the Empty Palaces: The Merchant Patrons of Modern Art in Pre-Revolutionary Russia* (New York: Universe Books, 1983), p. 58.

[42]Selivanovskij, "Očerki russkoj poèzii XX veka," p. 23; Selivanovskij, *Očerki po istorii russkoj sovetskoj poèzii*, pp. 49-50. Not always heeding his own aesthetic theories, Gumilev exhibited Symbolist tendencies in his partially derivative early verse and developed a marked Symbolist manner in his later writing. Sampson, *Gumilev*, pp. 342, 418-419.

[43]Pomorska, *Russian Formalist Theory*, pp. 47, 55, 66, 68; Žirmunskij, *Voprosy teorii literatury*, p. 177; Samurin, "Osnovnye tečenija," p, xxiii; Vladislav Xodasevič, *Nekropol'. Vospominanija* (Brussels: Les Éditions

122   NOTES

Petropolis, 1939), pp. 118–119.

[44]Konstantin Močul'skij, *Aleksandr Blok* (Paris: YMCA Press, 1948), p.
350.   Blok evidently saw no real difference between the Acmeists and the
Symbolists (as the latter were evolving at this time). *Ibid.*, p. 351. But he
failed to take into account differences in perception and in world view.

[45]Pomorska, *Russian Formalist Theory*, p. 65; Močul'skij, *Blok*, p. 350.

[46]Pomorska, *Russian Formalist Theory*, p. 52.

[47]*Ibid.*, p. 82; Žirmunskij, *Voprosy teorii literatury*, p. 188; Žirmunskij,
"Preodolevšie simvolizm," p. 53; V. Sovsun, "Akmeizm ili Adamizm,"
Literaturnaja ènciklopedija, Vol. I (Moscow: Izdatel'stvo Kommunističeskoj
Adademii, 1930.   Reprint Ann Arbor: American Council of Learned Societies
Reprints.   Russian Series No. 20, J. W. Edwards. Edwards Bros., Inc., 1948),
cols. 71–72; Ginzburg, *O lirike*, pp. 375–376.   Driver maintains that the
Acmeists were against a type of mysticism no longer characteristic of such
poets as Aleksandr Blok and Vjačeslav Ivanov.   Driver, "Acmeism," p. 145.
(Blok and Ivanov never repudiated mysticism, however.)   Struve notes that
the Acmeists were opposed to the efforts of Vjačeslav Ivanov and Andrej
Belyj to make Symbolism into something more than a poetic school.   Struve,
"Tvorčeskij put' Gumileva," pp. x–xi.   The Acmeists' acceptance of reality
was reflected in their poetic themes and use of visual images. Žirmunskij,
"Preodolevšie simvolizm," pp. 29–31; Selivanovskij, *Očerki po istorii russkoj
sovtskoj poèzii*, p. 49; Pomorska, *Russian Formalist Theory*, p. 46.

[48]L'vov–Rogačevskij, *Novejšaja russkaja literatura*, pp. 285–286.

[49]Struve, "O. È. Mandel'štam," p. xxxviii.

[50]V. Dynnik, "Akmeisty," *Bol'šaja sovetskaja ènciklopedija*, Vol. I
(Moscow: 1929), col. 824; Pozner, *La Littérature Russe*, p. 226; Žirmunskij,
"Preodolevšie simvolizm," p. 31.

[51]Dynnik, "Akmeisty," col. 824; Žirmunskij, "Preodolevšie simvolizm," p.
54.

[52]Mixail Kuzmin, "O prekrasnoj jasnosti," *Apollon*, No. 4 (1910), pp.
5–10.

[53]*Ibid.*, p. 10.   That Kuzmin links aesthetic perfection to clarity is evident
from the title of his essay.   Ljubov' Gurevič, *Literatura i èstetika* (Moscow:
Russkaja mysl', 1912), p. 123.   The following critics have discussed the
relationship between *Apollon* and Acmeism: Georgette Donchin, *The Influence
of French Symbolism on Russian Poetry* ('S–Gravenhage: Mouton and
Company, 1958), pp. 72–75; Denis Mickiewicz, "*Apollo* and Modernist Poetics,"
Russian Literature Triquarterly (Fall, 1971), pp. 244–245. Mickiewicz refers to
articles in *Apollon* by Bakst and Vološin which, insofar as supporting
classicism in art and criticizing Symbolism are concerned, predate the Acmeist
doctrine.   In an editorial statement published in *Apollon*, classicism was
advocated as a protest against "the formless daring of the creative work" in
which "the laws of cultural succession" had been forgotten. "Vstuplenie,"
Apollon, No. 1 (1910), p. 3. (Sergej Makovskij was the editor, but the article
was unsigned.)   While not initially an Acmeist journal, *Apollon* was
nevertheless the obvious vehicle for the Acmeist cause. It was the witness of
a change in orientation from Symbolism to Acmeism.   Donchin, *French
Symbolism*, p. 72.

[54]Driver, "Acmeism," p. 148.

[55]Žirmunskij, "Preodolevšie simvolizm," pp. 27–28 ff.; Pozner, *La
Littérature Russe*, pp. 224–225, 335; "Kuzmin, Mixail Alekseevič," *Bol'šaja
sovetskaja ènciklopedija*, Vol. XXXV (1st edition Moscow: 1937), col. 373;

Aničkov, *Novaja russkaja poèzija*, p. 62.

[56] Pomorska, *Russian Formalist Theory*, p. 46.

[57] Gleb Struve, "Tvorčeskij put' Gumileva," pp. xi–xii. Gleb Struve, Notes, in N. Gumilev, *Sobranie sočinenij v četyrex tomax*, edited by G. P. Struve and B. A. Filippov, Vol. IV (Washington, D.C.: Victor Kamkin, Inc., 1968), p. 599; Georgij Ivanov, Introduction, in N. S. Gumilev, *Pis'ma o russkoj poèzii* (Petrograd: Mysl', 1923), p. 5. Driver feels that the manifestoes, "despite shortcomings, gave expression to a point of view that had been developing for some time within the Symbolist movement." He feels that they were carelessly written, however. Driver, "Acmeism," pp. 142–143.

[58] N. S. Gumilev, "Nasledie simvolizma i akmeizm," *Pis'ma o russkoj poèzii* (Petrograd: Mysl', 1923), pp. 37–38. Driver feels that both Vjačeslav Ivanov and Aleksandr Blok, in their addresses before the Society of the Partisans of the Artistic Word, anticipated Gumilev in calling for attention to craftsmanship in poetry and a renewed interest in things of this world. Driver, "Acmeism," p. 145. They did not break with Symbolism, however, and they are more akin to well-meaning reformers than to literary revolutionaries.

[59] Gumilev, "Nasledie simvolizma i akmeizm," p. 38. Gleb Struve criticized deviations from logic in Gumilev's conception of Russian and Western European Symbolism. Gleb Struve, "Tvorčeskij put' Gumileva," p. xiii. Driver argues that Gumilev confuses mystical Symbolism with the Symbolist movement as a whole. Driver, "Acmeism," p. 149. Sergej Makovskij maintains, however, that Gumilev "called poets back to earthly reality." Makovskij, *Na Parnase serebrjanogo veka*, p. 217.

[60] Gumilev, "Nasledie simvolizma i akmeizm," p. 39. Gumilev emphasized the importance of the word as a "complex union of concrete and associative meanings." Robert Whittaker, Jr., "Translator's Preface (Nikolai Gumilev and Acmeist Criticism)," *Russian Literature Triquarterly* (Fall, 1971), p. 139.

[61] Gumilev, "Nasledie simvolizma i akmeizm," pp. 39–40.

[62] *Ibid.*, pp. 40–42. Driver feels that Gumilev was never able to shake off his belief that the poet is a superior being, "if not 'priestly,' then a leader with great powers." Driver, "Acmeism," p. 151. This would suggest that the poet has access to knowledge denied to others. While this pose is characteristic of Gumilev in his personal life, it is not part of his program for Acmeism.

[63] Gumilev, "Nasledie simvolizma i akmeizm," p. 42. Gumilev wrote that these names were often "uttered" in circles "close to Acmeism." His remark would imply that there had been a great deal of discussion involving these names, so much, in fact, that even those poets peripheral to the Acmeist movement ("close to Acmeism") would have mentioned them frequently. Neither Gorodeckij nor Mandel'štam, however, refers to them. Gumilev may well have cited them to establish an authority for Acmeism, attempting also to posit Acmeism as a leader of its age, for each of the writers he cites represents a great age of literature.

[64] Driver feels that Gumilev's essay was the more important of the two, since Gorodeckij's is primarily an elaboration of some of Gumilev's remarks. Driver, "Acmeism," p. 152. In spite of the apparent agreement and cooperation between the two, to which the joint publication of their essays would seem to attest, there had evidently been some friction between them. Chalsma, *Russian Acmeism*, p. 47; Gleb Struve, "Tvorčeskij put' Gumileva," p. xvi.

[65] Sergej Gorodeckij, "Nekotorye tečenija v sovremennoj russkoj poèzii,"

Apollon, No. 1 (1913), pp. 46–47. Gorodeckij remarked in passing that " . . . Annenskij was not crowned by them [the Symbolists]," thereby implying that the Acmeists alone had really appreciated his poetic and critical talents. Brjusov scorned Gorodeckij's assessment of the downfall of Symbolism. Valerij Brjusov, "Novye tečenija v russkoj poèzll. Akmeizm," *Russkaju mysl'*, No. 4 (1913), p. 137. Močul'skij declared that Gorodeckij's remarks did not apply to a single contemporary Symbolist. Močul'skij, *Aleksandr Blok*, p. 349; surely Gorodeckij's comments would be pertinent as far as both Belyj and Blok were concerned.

[66]Gorodeckij, "Novye tečenija," p. 48.

[67]*Ibid.*, pp. 48–49.

[68]Irina Bušman, *Poètičeskoe iskusstvo Mandel'štama* (Munich: Institut po izučeniju SSSR, 1964), p. 56; Gleb Struve, "O. È. Mandel'štam," p. lxxx.

[69]Gleb Struve, "O. È. Mandel'štam," p. xxxviii; Clarence Brown, "Mandelshtam's Acmeist Manifesto. Translated from the Russian with a Note. Osip Mandelshtam, 'The Morning of Acmeism,'" *The Russian Review*, Vol. 24, No. 1 (January–October, 1965), p. 46.

[70]Osip Mandel'štam, "Utro akmeizma," in Osip Mandel'štam, *Sobranie sočinenij v dvux tomax*, edited by G. P. Struve and B. A. Filippov, Vol. II (New York: Inter-Language Literary Associates, 1966), p. 362. "Utro akmeizma" was first published in *Sirena*, Nos. 4–5 (30 January, 1919), pp. 69–74. Gleb Struve and B. A. Filippov, Notes, in Osip Mandel'štam, *Sobranie sočinenij v dvux tomax*, edited by G. P. Struve and B. A. Filippov, Vol. II (New York: Inter-Language Literary Associates, 1966), p. 608.

[71]Mandel'štam, "Utro Akmeizma," pp. 362–363. Nils Åke Nilsson feels that Mandel'štam had more interest in the word *per se* than did the other Acmeists. Nils Åke Nilsson, "Osip Mandel'štam and his Poetry," *Scando-Slavica*, Vol. IX (1963), p. 45.

[72]Mandel'štam, "Utro Akmeizma," p. 363.

[73]*Ibid.*, pp. 364–365. The Acmeists were not really "stay-at-homes" in the literal sense; Gumilev visited Ethiopia and Western Europe, many of his poems reflecting his interest in "exotic" lands. Axmatova also travelled to the West. Mandel'štam did not, of course, condemn interest in other cultures; rather, he was criticizing the Symbolists' tendencies to escape physical reality and seek to transcend earthly existence.

[74]*Ibid.*, p. 365.

[75]*Ibid.*, p. 366.

[76]*Ibid.*, p. 366.

[77]Mandel'štam is the only Acmeist to allude to music. His admiration for Bach must have resulted from the composer's emphasis on structure. Perhaps Bach represents musically what the cathedral signifies architecturally. Unlike Gumilev, who established literary models for the Acmeists, Mandel'štam did not mention other writers, referring instead to architecture and Bach. Mandel'štam's lyric "Žil Aleksandr Gercovič" ("There Lived Aleksandr Gercovič") is about a musician and is constructed like a musical composition: the name "Aleksandr Gercovič" is a "major chord." Mandel'štam repeats it in variations ("Aleksandr Skercovič," "Aleksandr Serdcevič," "Aleksandr Skercevič") at the middle and end of the poem. The very variations of the name are significant musically, with "Skercovič" and "Skercevič" equivalent to "scherzo." "Serdcevič" is from "serdce," "heart," symbolic of the emotional aspect of music. The subject of the poem was a musician neighbor. See Osip Mandel'štam, "Žil Aleksandr Cercovič," in Osip Mandel'štam, *Sobranie*

sočinenij v trex tomax, edited by G. P. Struve and B. A. Filippov, Vol. I
(2nd edition Washington, D.C.: Inter-Language Literary Associates, 1967), pp.
162-163.

[78]Mandel'štam, "Utro Akmeizma," p. 367.

[79]*Ibid.,* p. 367.

[80]*Ibid.,* p. 367.

CHAPTER SIX

[1]A number of critics have acknowledged Annenskij's role as mentor to
the Acmeists. They include: Vladimir Pjast [Pestovskij], *Vstreči* (Moscow:
Federacija, 1929), pp. 137-138; A. I. Pavlovskij, *Anna Axmatova. očerk
tvorčestva* (Leningrad: Lenizdat, 1966), pp. 69-70; Boris Éjxenbaum, *Anna
Axmatova. opyt analiza* (Petrograd: Petropečat', 1923), p. 25; A. Fedorov,
"Poètičeskoe tvorčestvo Innokentija Annenskogo," Innokentij Annenskij,
Stixotvorenija i tragedii (Leningrad: Sovetskij pisatel', 1959), pp. 17-21;
Georgij Adamovič, "Pamjati Annenskogo," *Cex poètov,* II-III (Berlin: 1922),
pp. 92-93; Georgij Adamovič, "Annenskij i Gumilev," *Novoe russkoe slovo*
(New York: 2 May, 1965), p. 3; Johannes Holthusen, *Studien zur Äesthetik
und Poetik des russischen Symbolismus* (Göttingen: Vandenhoeck and
Ruprecht, 1957), pp. 52-53; Eridano Bazzarelli, *La Poesia di Innokentij
Annenskij* (Milan: U. Mursia, 1965), p. 19; Howard William Chalsma, *Russian
Acmeism: Its History, Doctrine and Poetry* (Seattle: University of
Washington Dissertation, 1967), pp. 1, 23-24 ff.; Catherine Nebolsine Coulter,
Aspects of the Poetry of Innokentij Annenskij (New York: Columbia
University Master's Essay, 1966), p. 1; Vladimir Markov and Merrill Sparks,
Modern Russian Poetry (Indianapolis: Bobbs-Merrill Company, Inc., 1967), p.
lix; Vsevolod Setchkarev, *Studies in the Life and Work of Innokentij Annenskij*
(The Hague: Mouton and Company, 1963), p. 5. Other critics have mentioned
the link between Annenskij and the Acmeists: V. A. Nikonov, "Annenskij,
Innokentij Fedorovič," *Kratkaja literaturnaja ènciklopedija,* Vol. I (Moscow:
Sovetskaja ènciklopedija, 1962), col. 237; Ju. Ivask, "Četyre kritika," *Novoe
russkoe slovo* (New York: 1 March, 1953), p. 8; Kornej Čukovskij, "Innokentij
Annenskij," *Reč',* No. 336 (7 December, 1909), p. 4.

[2]For Annenskij's and the Acmeists' association with Tsarskoe Selo, see
the following: Fedorov, "Poètičeskoe tvorčestvo Annenskogo," p. 6. Peter
Russell, "A Note on Osip Emilievitch Mandelshtam," *Delta* (January, 1959),
pp. 1-2; N. Punin, "Problema žizni v poèzii Annenskogo," *Apollon,* No. 10
(1914), pp. 47-48; Nikolaj Ocup, *Dnevnik v stixax* (Paris: 1950), pp. 102-103;
Ju. Lerner, ed., *Tsarskoe Selo v poèzii,* with an essay by È. F. Gollerbax (St.
Petersburg: Parfenon, 1922), p. 11; Jeanne Rude, *Anna Akhmatova* (Paris:
Éditions Seghers, 1968), p. 12. Annenskij had a close relationship with his
students and was drawn to young people. L.[jubov'] G.[urevič], "Pamjati I. F.
Annenskogo," *Russkaja mysl',* No. 1, Pt. II (1910), pp. 163, 166; Ar. Muxin,
"I. F. Annenskij (Nekrolog)," *Germes,* No. 20 (15 December, 1909), p. 609; V.
N. Il'in, "Innokentij Annenskij i konec Periklova veka Rossii," *Vozroždenie,* no.
166 (Paris: October, 1965), p. 45; Vladimir Pozner, *Panorama de la
Littérature Russe Contemporaine* (Paris: Kra, 1929), pp. 41-42; A. Ja.
Golovin, *Vstreči i vpečatlenija. Vospominanija xudožnika,* edited by and with
the commentary of È. F. Gollerbax (Moscow-Leningrad: Iskusstvo, 1940), p.
99.

[3]Anna Axmatova, "V Tsarskom Sele, III," Anna Axmatova, *Sočinenija,*
edited by G. P. Struve and B. A. Filippov, Vol. I (2nd edition New York:

Inter-Language Literary Associates, 1967), pp. 63–64.

[4]D. S. Mirsky, *A History of Russian Literature: from its Beginnings to 1900*, edited by Francis J. Whitfield (New York: Vintage Books, Alfred A. Knopf, Inc., 1958), p. 83.

[5]Gleb Struve, "N. S. Gumilev. Žizn' i ličnost'," in N. Gumilev, *Sobranie sočinenij v četyrex tomax*, edited by G. P. Struve and B. A. Filippov, Vol. I (Washington, D.C.: Victor Kamkin, Inc., 1962), p. x.

[6]Jurij Annenkov, *Dnevnik moix vstreč. Cikl tragedij*, Vol. I (New York: Inter-Language Literary Associates, 1966), p. 105.

[7]Marie Maline, *Nicolas Gumilev: Poète et critique acméiste* (Brussels: Palais des Académies, 1964), p. 13. According to Sergej Makovskij, Annenskij and Gumilev were not on close terms at this time. Sergej Makovskij, "Nikolaj Gumilev po ličnym vospominanijam," *Novyj žurnal*, No. 77 (New York: 1964), p. 159. Makovskij contradicts himself elsewhere, stating that Gumilev "spoke enthusiastically" about Annenskij. Sergej Makovskij, *Na Parnase serebrjanogo veka* (Munich: Verlag ZOPE, 1962), p. 198.

[8]Maline, *Gumilev*, p. 14; Setchkarev, *Annenskij*, pp. 36–37.

[9]Leonid Strakhovsky, *Craftsmen of the Word: Three Poets of Modern Russia* (Cambridge: Harvard University Press, 1949. 2nd edition Westport, Connecticut: Greenwood Press, 1969), pp. 15–16; M. A. Beketova, *Aleksandr Blok: biografičeskij očerk* (Petersburg: Alkonost, 1922. Reprint The Hague: Mouton and Company, 1969), p. 125; Makovskij, "Gumilev po ličnym vospominanijam," p. 167; Makovskij, *Portrety sovremennikov*, p. 243. The 3 December, 1911 meeting of the "Obščestvo revnitelej xudožestvennogo slova" ("Society of the Partisans of the Artistic Word") was devoted to Annenskij. See Valerian Čudovskij, "Literaturnaja žizn'," *Russkaja xudožestvennaja letopis'*, No. 20 (December, 1911), p. 321.

[10]Aleksej N. Tolstoj, "N. Gumilev," *Poslednie novosti*, No. 467 (Paris: 23 October, 1921), p. 2; Gleb Struve, "N. S. Gumilev. žizn' i ličnost'," N. Gumilev, *Sobranie sočinenij v četyrex tomax*, edited by G. P. Struve and B. A. Filippov, Vol. I (Washington, D.C.: Victor Kamkin, Inc., 1962), p. xiv; Chalsma, *Acmeism*, p. 24; Coulter, *Annenskij*, p. 2.

[11]Makovskij, "Gumilev po ličnym vospominanijam," pp. 163–164. Both V. N. Il'in and D. Blagoj discuss the tie between Annenskij and *Apollon*. V. N. Il'in, "Innokentij Annenskij i konec Periklova veka Rossii," *Vozroždenie*, No. 166 (Paris: October, 1965), p. 46; D. Blagoj, "Annenskij Innokentij Fedorovič," *Literaturnaja ènciklopedija*, Vol. I (Moscow: Izdatel'stvo Kommunističeskoj Akademii, 1930. Ann Arbor: American Council of Learned Societies Reprints. Russian Series No. 20, J. W. Edwards, Edwards Bros., Inc., 1948), col. 166.

[12]*Apollon*, No. 3 (December, 1909), p. 48.

[13]Nikolaj Gumilev, "Innokentij Annenskij, 'Kiparisovyj larec,' i drugie," *Pis'ma o russkoj poèzii* (Petrograd: Mysl', 1923), p. 88.

[14]Jurij Verxovskij, "Put' poèta. O poèzii N. S. Gumileva," *Sovremennaja literatura* (Leningrad: Mysl', 1925), pp. 114–115. Blagoj felt that Annenskij shared with the Parnassians a love for the intrinsic value of the word. D. Blagoj, "Annenskij, Innokentij Fedorovič," *Literaturnaja ènciklopedija*, Vol. I (Moscow: Izdatel'stvo Kommunističeskoj Akademii, 1930. Ann Arbor: American Council of Learned Societies Reprints. Russian Series No. 20, J. W. Edwards, Edwards Bros., Inc., 1948), cols. 165–166. Annenskij's translations of the Parnassians and Symbolists, "Parnascy i prokljatye" ("The Parnassians and Accursed Ones"), were appended to *Tixie pesni* (*Quiet Songs*).

[15]Setchkarev, *Annenskij*, pp. 38–39. Gumilev's interest in the Parnassians can be seen from his list of four writers in which Gautier's name is included. N. S. Gumilev, "Nasledie simvolizma i akmeizm," *Pis'ma o russkoj poèzii* (Petrograd: Mysl', 1923), p. 42. Blagoj, "Annenskij," cols. 165–166. For the Acmeists' views on the intrinsic value of the word, see the discussion of their essays in Chapter Five. The Acmeists stressed the fact that poetry (art) is essentially a craft rather than a religious experience and emphasized the role of conscious creativity, a factor important for Annenskij as well.

[16]Gleb Struve, *Russkaja literatura v izgnanii* (New York: Chekhov Publishing House, 1956), p. 321. But Struve fails to develop his argument. Bazzarelli, too, spoke of but did not analyze differences between the two poets. Bazzarelli, *Annenskij*, p. 15.

[17]Georgij Adamovič, "Annenskij i Gumilev," *Novoe russkoe slovo* (New York: 2 May, 1965), p. 3.

[18]Gleb Struve, "Anna Akhmatova," Anna Axmatova, *Sočinenija*, edited by G. P. Struve and B. A. Filippov, Vol. I (2nd edition New York: Inter–Language Literary Associates, 1967), p. 5; Jeanne Rude, *Anna Akhmatova* (Paris: Éditions Seghers, 1968), p. 9. Axmatova considered Acmeism to have been founded at Tsarskoe Selo. *Ibid.*, p. 63.

[19]V. V. Vejdle, "Peterburgskaja poètika," N. Gumilev, *Sobranie sočinenij v četyrex tomax*, edited by G. P. Struve and B. A. Filippov, Vol. IV (Washington, D.C.: Victor Kamkin, Inc., 1968), p. xv.

[20]Nikita Struve, "Vosem' časov s Annoj Axmatovoj," Anna Axmatova, *Sočinenija*, edited by G. P. Struve and B. A. Filippov, Vol. II (New York: Inter–Language Literary Associates, 1968), pp. 339–340.

[21]Gollerbax, *Tsarskoe Selo v poèzii*, pp. 13–14. There were, to be sure, stylistic differences between the two poets. Georgij Čulkov, "Zakatnyj zvon (I. Annenskij i Anna Axmatova)," *Otkliki. Literatura. Iskusstvo.* Nauka., No. 9 (1914), (Supplement to newspaper *Den'*), pp. 2–3.

[22]Irina Bušman, *Poètičeskoe iskusstvo Mandel'štama* (Munich: Institut po izučeniju SSSR, 1964), p. 68; Gollerbax, *Tsarskoe Selo v poèzii*, p. 14.

[23]Osip Mandel'štam, "O prirode slova," Osip Mandel'štam, *Sobranie sočinenij v dvux tomax*, edited by G. P. Struve and B. A. Filippov, Vol. II (New York: Inter–Language Literary Associates, 1966), pp. 294–295. Nadežda Mandel'štam repeatedly stressed Mandel'štam's debt to Annenskij. Nadežda Mandel'štam, *Vtoraja kniga* (Paris: YMCA Press, 1972), pp. 37, 93, 127, 134, 391, 435, and 513. With the verse of Gumilev and Axmatova and a few other books, the poems of Annenskij were virtually the only works of twentieth–century Russian literature that the Mandel'štams owned, thus attesting to the high regard Mandel'štam had for Annenskij. Nadežda Mandel'štam, *Vospominanija* (New York: Chekhov Publishing House, 1970), p. 255.

[24]He considered the psychological emphases in Axmatova's poems to be only a vulgarization of Annenskij's methods. Osip Mandel'štam, "Burja i natisk," Osip Mandel'štam, *Sobranie sočinenij v dvux tomax*, edited by G. P. Struve and B. A. Filippov, Vol. II (New York: Inter–Language Literary Associates, 1966), pp. 386–387. Semen Karlinskij, "Veščestvennost' Annenskogo," *Novyj žurnal*, No. 85 (New York: December, 1966), p. 70.

[25]For an analysis of these lyrics, see Chapter Two.

[26]Setchkarev, *Annenskij*, pp. 70–71.

[27]Karlinskij, "Veščestvennost' Annenskogo," p. 73; Georgij Mejer, "Sergej Makovskij i Serebrjanyj vek," *Grani*, No. 54 (Frankfurt: 1963), p. 209. In

his lyric "Čelovek," *Stixotvorenija i tragedii*, p. 146, Annenskij argued that the poet, not chosen by some higher force, invented himself.

[28]Fedorov, "Poètičeskoe tvorčestvo Annenskogo," pp. 17, 20–23; A. Evgen'ev, "Stixotvorenija Innokentija Annenskogo," *Literaturnoe obozrenie*, No. 14 (1939), p. 32.

[29]Sam Driver, "Anna Akhmatova: Early Love Poems," *Russian Literature Triquarterly* (Fall, 1971), p. 299.

[30]Gumilev, "Nasledie simvolizma i akmeizm," p. 42; Osip Mandel'štam, "Utro Akmeizma," Osip Mandel'štam, *Sobranie sočinenij v dvux tomax*, edited by G. P. Struve and B. A. Filippov, Vol. II (New York: Inter–Language Literary Associates, 1966), p. 365. Mandel'štam uses architectural motifs in his verse, for example, in *Kamen'* (*Stone*). For a discussion of architectural motifs in Mandel'štam, see Viktor Žirmunskij, *Voprosy teorii literatury (stat'i 1916–1926)* (Leningrad: 1928. Reprint 'S-Gravenhage: Mouton and Company, 1962), pp. 327–329. For Mandel'štam, architecture represented a significant component in Western civilization. Ryszard Przybylski has discussed the intellectual facets of Mandel'štam's verse in "Arkadia Osipa Mandelsztama," *Slavica Orientalis*, No. 3 (1964), p. 243. Axmatova shared this interest in architecture as well; see Leonid Grossman, *Mastera slova* (Moscow: 1928), p. 308. Kuzmin, a transitional figure between Symbolism and Acmeism, equated the writer and architect in "O prekrasnoj jasnosti," *Apollon*, No. 4 (1910), p. 10.

[31]Ginzburg, *O lirike*, pp. 362–363. Annenskij stressed the importance of concrete objects in "Poètu," *Stixotvorenija i tragedii*, pp. 219–220.

[32]D. S. Mirsky, *A History of Russian Literature. II. After 1881*, edited and abridged by Francis J. Whitfield (New York: Alfred A. Knopf, 1949), p. 448. The following critics have commented on Annenskij's use of prosaisms and everyday language: Jurij Ivask, "Slučevskij," *Novyj žurnal*, No. 79 (New York: June, 1965, p. 280; Bazzarelli, *Annenskij*, p. 126; Evgenij Arxippov, "Nikto i Ničej. Lirika Innokentija Annenskogo," *Mirtovyj venec* (Moscow: Žatva, 1915), p. 80; A. Fedorov, "Innokentij Annenskij," *Stixotvorenija Innokentija Annenskogo* (Leningrad: Sovetskij pisatel', 1939), p. 23; Lubov Alex Shapovaloff, *The Aesthetics and Poetics of Innokentij Annenskij* (Seattle: University of Washington Dissertation, 1968), p. 315; Coulter, *Annenskij*, pp. 19, 21–22. Axmatova also uses everyday language. Žirmunskij, "Preodolevšie simvolizm," p. 33; Rude, *Akhmatova*, p. 77.

[33]Like Annenskij's emphasis on time, his use of conversational elements and prosaisms points to a rejection of mysticism and incomprehensibility and an acceptance of reality. While Blok, for example, employed elements of the "častuška" or street song in "Dvenadcat'" ("The Twelve"), (see Ginzburg, *O lirike*, pp. 315–316), his use of conversational vocabulary did not create an impression of clarity. Given the non-rational basis of late Symbolist poetry, the use of prosaisms only heightened estrangement from the physical world. For the Symbolists, states Viktor Gofman, an original "fetishization" of the word is characteristic. Viktor Gofman, "Jazyk simvolistov," *Literaturnoe nasledstvo*, Vol. 27–28 (Moscow: Žurnal'no–gazetnoe ob"edinenie, 1937), p. 60.

[34]Annenskij underscores this concept in the lyric "Poètu" ("To the Poet"), in which logic directs the course of art.

[35]Shapovaloff, *Annenskij*, pp. 223, 332; Boris Larin, "O Kiparisovom larce," *Literaturnaja mysl'*, No. 2 (1922–1923), p. 152. Other critics have felt that Annenskij shunned clarity, favoring ambiguity. Pozner, *La Littérature Russe*, pp. 26–27. Annenskij's complexity should not be confused with ambiguity.

[36]Mandel'štam, "Utro akmeizma," p. 366. Logical sentence structure was important for Axmatova. See Alexis Rannit, "Anna Akhmatova Considered in a Context of Art Nouveau," Anna Axmatova, *Sočinenija*, edited by G. P. Struve and B. A. Filippov, Vol. II (New York: Inter-Language Literary Associates, 1968), p. 37. Logic was not significant for the later Symbolists. Žirmunskij, "Preodolevšie simvolizm," p. 29.

[37]Chalsma, *Acmeism*, p. 25; Shapovaloff, *Annenskij*, p. 274.

[38]"Annenskij, Innokentij Fedorovič," *Malaja sovetskaja ènciklopedija*, Vol. I (Moscow: 1930), col. 335; Innokentij Annenskij, "Stixotvorenija Ja. P. Polonskogo kak pedagogičeskij material," *Vospitanie i obučenie*, No. 6 (June, 1887), p. 138.

[39]Innokentij Annenskij, "Bal'mont lirik," *Kniga otraženij* (St. Petersburg: Bašmačnikov Brothers, 1906. Reprint Munich: Wilhelm Fink Verlag, 1969), pp. 171-172.

[40]Mandel'štam, "Utro akmeizma," p. 362.

[41]Innokentij Annenskij, "Pedagogičeskie pis'ma. pervoe pis'mo. Jazyki v srednej škole," *Russkaja škola*, Nos. 7-8 (1892), p. 165.

[42]Gumilev, "Nasledie simvolizma i akmeizm," p. 39.

APPENDIX

[1]Anna Axmatova, "Sžala ruki pod temnoj vual'ju," Anna Axmatova, *Sočinenija*, Edited by G. P. Struve and B. A. Filippov, Vol. I (2nd edition New York: Inter-Language Literary Associates, 1967), pp. 64-65.

[2]"Muza," *Ibid.*, p. 230.

[3]"Pustyx nebes prozračnoe steklo," *Ibid.*, p. 130.

[4]"Sad," *Ibid.*, p. 73.

[5]"V Tsarskom Sele, Pt. III, Smuglyj otrok brodil po allejam," *Ibid.*, pp. 63-64.

[6]Nikolaj Gumilev, "Osennjaja pesnja," N. Gumilev, *Sobranie sočinenij v četyrex tomax*, edited by G. P. Struve and B. A. Filippov, Vol. I (Washington, D.C.: Victor Kamkin, Inc., 1962), pp. 17-18.

[7]"Piza," *Ibid.*, pp. 225-226.

[8]Osip Mandel'štam, "V Petropole prozračnom my umrem," Osip Mandel'štam, *Sobranie sočinenij v četyrex tomax*, edited by G. P. Struve and B. A. Filippov, Vol. I (Washington, D.C.: Inter-Language Literary Associates, 1967), p. 61.

[9]"V Peterburge my sojdemsja snova," *Ibid.*, pp. 85-86.

BIBLIOGRAPHY

BOOKS AND COLLECTED WORKS
BY INNOKENTIJ ANNENSKIJ AND THE ACMEISTS

Annenskij, Innokentij. *Kniga otraženij.* (St. Petersburg: Bašmačnikov Brothers, 1906. Reprint Munich: Wilhelm Fink Verlag, 1969).

_____. *Puškin i Tsarskoe Selo.* (St. Petersburg: Šumaxer Brothers, 1899; first given as a speech at Tsarskoe Selo, 26 May, 1899).

_____. *Stixotvorenija.* (Leningrad: Sovetskij pisatel', 1939.

_____. *Stixotvorenija i tragedii.* (Leningrad: Sovetskij pisatel', 1959).

_____. *Teatr Evripida.* (St. Petersburg: 1907. 2nd edition, Vols. I–III, Moscow: 1916–1921).

_____. *'Vakxanki,' tragedija Evripida.* (St. Petersburg: 1894).

_____. *Vtoraja kniga otraženij.* (St. Petersburg: Bašmačnikov Brothers, 1909. Reprint Munich: Wilhelm Fink Verlag, 1969).

Axmatova, Anna. *Sočinenija.* Edited by G. P. Struve and B. A. Filippov. Vol. I. (2nd edition New York: Inter–Language Literary Associates, 1967).

_____. *Sočinenija.* Edited by G. P. Struve and B. A. Filippov. Vol. II. (New York: Inter–Language Literary Associates, 1968).

Gumilev, N.S. *Pis'ma o russkoj poèzii.* (Petrograd: Mysl', 1923).

_____. *Sobranie sočinenij v četyrex tomax.* Edited by G. P. Struve and B. A. Filippov, Vol. I. (Washington, D.C.: Victor Kamkin, Inc., 1962).

_____. *Sobranie sočinenij v četyrex tomax.* Edited by G. P. Struve and B. A. Filippov. Vol. II. (Washington, D.C.: Victor Kamkin, Inc., 1964).

_____. *Sobranie sočinenij v četyrex tomax.* Edited by G. P. Struve and B. A. Filippov. Vol. III. (Washington, D.C.: Victor Kamkin, Inc., 1966).

_____. *Sobranie sočinenij v četyrex tomax.* Edited by G. P. Struve and B. A. Filippov. Vol. IV. (Washington, D.C.: Victor Kamkin, Inc., 1968).

Mandel'štam, Osip. *Sobranie sočinenij v dvux tomax.* Edited by G. P. Struve and B. A. Filippov. Vol. II. (New York: Inter–Language Literary Associates, 1966).

_____. *Sobranie sočinenij v trex tomax.* Edited by G. P. Struve and B. A. Filippov. Vol. I. (2nd edition Washington, D.C.: Inter–Language Literary Associates, 1967).

_____. *Sobranie sočinenij v trex tomax.* Edited by G. P. Struve and B. A. Filippov. Vol. III. (New York: Inter–Language Literary Associates, 1969).

_____. *The Complete Prose and Letters.* Edited by Jane Gary Harris. Translated by Jane Gary Harris and Constance Link. (Ann Arbor: Ardis, 1979).

ARTICLES BY INNOKENTIJ ANNENSKIJ
AND THE ACMEISTS

Annenskij, Innokentij.   "A. N. Majkov i pedagogičeskoe značenie ego poèzii." *Russkaja škola*, No. 2 (February, 1898), pp. 40–61; No. 3 (March, 1898), pp. 53–66.

_____.   "Antičnaja tragedija." *Mir Božij* (November, 1902), pp. 1–41.

_____.   "Antičnyj mif v sovremennoj francuzskoj poèzii." *Germes*, No. 7 (1908), pp. 177–185; No. 8 (1908), pp. 209–213; No. 9 (1908), pp. 236–240; and No. 10 (1908), pp. 270–288.

_____.   "Čto takoe poèzija." posmertnaja stat'ja.   *Apollon*, No. 6 (1911), pp. 51–57.

_____.   "Èstetika *Mertvyx duš* i ee nasled'e."   *Apollon*, No. 8 (1911), pp. 50–58.

_____.   "Gončarov i ego Oblomov."   *Russkaja škola*, No. 4 (April, 1892), pp. 71–95.

_____.   "Iz nabljudenij nad jazykom i poèziej russkogo Severa," *Sbornik v čest' V. I. Lamanskogo* (St. Petersburg: 1883), pp. 196–211.

_____.   "Iz nabljudenij nad jazykom Likofrona," *Commentationes philologicae, sbornik statej v čest' Ivana Vasil'eviča Pomjalovskogo* (St. Petersburg: 1897), pp. 55–80.

_____.   "O formax fantastičeskogo u Gogolja."   *Russkaja škola*, No. 12 (December, 1890), pp. 93–104.

_____.   "O sovremennom lirizme."   'Oni,' Pt. 1.   *Apollon*, No. 1 (October, 1909), pp. 12–42; 'Oni,' Pt. 2.   *Apollon*, No. 2 (November, 1909), pp. 3–29; 'One.' *Apollon*, No. 3 (December, 1909), pp. 5–29.

_____.   "Ob èstetičeskom otnošenii Lermontova k prirode."   *Russkaja škola*, No. 12 (December, 1891), pp. 73–83.

_____.   "Obrazovatel'noe značenie rodnogo jazyka."   *Russkaja škola*, No. 1 (January, 1890), pp. 21–44.

_____.   "Pedagogičeskie pis'ma."   *Russkaja škola*, Nos. 7–8 (July–August, 1892), pp. 146–167; No. 11 (November, 1892), pp. 65–86; No. 2 (February, 1895), pp. 87–103.

_____.   "Sočinenija gr. A. K. Tolstogo kak pedagogičeskij material." *Vospitanie i obučenie*, No. 8 (August, 1887), pp. 181–191.

_____.   "Stixotvorenija Ja. P. Polonskogo kak pedagogičeskij material." *Vospitanie i obučenie*, No. 5 (May, 1887), pp. 109–118; No. 6 (June, 1887), pp. 133–142.

_____.   "Tragičeskaja Medeja."   *Žurnal Ministerstva narodnogo prosveščenija*, No. 8 (1903), pp. 358–367; No. 10 (1903), pp. 479–480; No. 11 (1903), pp. 481–514.

_____.   "Xudožestvennyj idealizm Gogolja."   *Russkaja škola*, No. 2 (February, 1902), pp. 114–125.

Gorodeckij, Sergej.   "*Čužoe nebo*. N. Gumileva. Review."   *Rec'*, No. 283 (October 15, 1912), p. 5.

_____.   "Nekotorye tečenija v sovremennoj russkoj poèzii."   *Apollon*, No. 1 (1913), pp. 46–50.

_____.   "Strana Reveransov i ee purpurno–lilovyj Bedeker."   *Protiv tečenija*, No. 1 (October 15, 1910), p. 3.

Kuzmin, Mixail.   "O prekrasnoj jasnosti."   *Apollon*, No. 4 (1910), pp. 5–10.

OTHER WORKS IN RUSSIAN

Adamovič, Georgij. *Odinočestvo i svoboda.* (New York: Chekhov Publishing House, 1955).

Agushi, Irène. *The Poetry of Georgij Ivanov.* (Cambridge, Massachusetts: Radcliffe College Dissertation, 1960).

Ajxenval'd, Julij. *Siluèty russkix pisatelej.* (Berlin: Slovo, 1923. Reprint The Hague: Mouton and Company, 1969).

Aničkov, E. *Novaja russkaja poèzija.* (Berlin: I. P. Ladyžnikov, 1922. Reprint The Hague: Mouton and Company, 1969).

Annenkov, Jurij. *Dnevnik moix vstreč. Cikl tragedij.* Vol. I. (New York: Inter-Language Literary Associates, 1966).

Beketova, M. A. *Aleksandr Blok: Biografičeskij očerk.* (Petersburg: Alkonost, 1922. Reprint The Hague: Mouton and Company, 1969).

Belyj, Andrej. *Arabeski.* (Moscow: 1911. Reprint Munich: Wilhelm Fink Verlag, 1969).

_____. *Načalo veka.* (Moscow-Leningrad: State Publishing House of belles-lettres, 1933).

_____. *Simvolizm.* (Moscow: Russkoe Tovariščestvo, 1910. Reprint Munich: Wilhelm Fink Verlag, 1969).

_____. *Stixotvorenija i poèmy.* (Moscow-Leningrad: Sovetskij pisatel', 1966).

Bicilli, P. M. *Kratkaja istorija russkoj literatury.* (Sofia: N.N. Alekseev, 1934).

Brjusov, Valerij. *Dalekie i blizkie.* (Moscow: Skorpion, 1912).

Bušman, Irina. *Poètičeskoe iskusstvo Mandel'štama.* (Munich: Institut po izučeniju SSSR, 1964).

Bušmin, A. S., ed. *Istorija russkoj literatury. Literatura 1890–1917 godov.* Vol. X. (Moscow-Leningrad: Akademija Nauk SSSR, 1954).

Cexnovicer, Orest. *Literatura i mirovaja vojna. 1914–1918.* (Moscow: Goslitizdat, 1938).

Čulkov, Georgij. *Gody stranstvij. Iz knigi vospominanij.* (Moscow: Federacija, 1930).

Dobin, E. S. *Poèzija Anny Axmatovoj.* (Leningrad: Sovetskij pisatel', 1968).

Èjxenbaum, Boris. *Anna Axmatova. opyt analiza.* (Petrograd: Petropečat', 1923).

Èrenburg, Il'ja. *Ljudi, gody, žizn'.* Bk. 2. (Moscow: Sovetskij pisatel', 1961).

Ežov I. S. and Šamurin, E. I. *Russkaja poèzija XX veka.* (Moscow: 1925).

Fidler, F. *Pervye literaturnye šagi.* (Moscow: 1911).

Ginzburg, L. Ja. *O lirike.* (Moscow-Leningrad: Sovetskij pisatel', 1964).

Golovin, A. Ja. *Vstreči i vpečatleniją. Vospominanija xudožnika.* Edited by and with the commentary of E. F. Gollerbax. (Moscow-Leningrad: Iskusstvo, 1940).

Gromov, Pavel. *A. Blok. Ego predšestvenniki i sovremenniki.* (Moscow-Leningrad: Sovetskij pisatel', 1966).

Grossman, Leonid. *Mastera slova.* (Moscow: 1928).

Gurevič, Ljubov'. *Literatura i èstetika.* (Moscow: Russkaja mysl', 1912).

Ivanov, Georgij. *Peterburgskie zimy.* (New York: Chekhov Publishing House, 1952).

Jablonko, B. P. *I. F. Annenskij (k tridcatiletiju so dnja smerti).* (Baku: Izdatel'stvo Narkomprosa Azerbajdžanskoj SSR, 1940).

Krutikova, N. E. and Kruk, I. T., ed. *Russkaja literatura XX veka. dooktjabr'skij period.* (Kiev: Višča škola, 1970).

Lerner, Ju., ed. *Tsarskoe Selo v poèzii.* With an essay by È. F. Gollerbax. (St. Petersburg: Parfenon, 1922).

L'vov–Rogačevskij, Vasilij. *Novejšaja russkaja literatura.* (3rd edition Moscow–Leningrad: L. D. Frenkel', 1924).

Makovskij, Sergej. *Na Parnase serebrjanogo veka.* (Munich: Verlag ZOPE, 1962).

──────. *Portrety sovremennikov.* (New York: Chekhov Publishing House, 1955).

Mandel'štam, Nadežda. *Vospominanija.* (New York: Chekhov Publishing House, 1970).

──────. *Vtoraja kniga.* (Paris: YMCA Press, 1972).

Močul'skij, Konstantin. *Aleksandr Blok.* (Paris: YMCA Press, 1948).

──────. *Andrej Belyj.* (Paris: YMCA Press, 1955).

Ocup, Nikolaj. *Dnevnik v stixax.* (Paris: 1950).

──────. *Sovremenniki.* (Paris: Imprimerie Cooperative Étoile, 1961).

Ovsjaniko–Kulikovskij, Dmitrij. *Istorija russkoj literatury XIX veka.* Vol. V. (Moscow: 1911).

Pavlovskij, A. I. *Anna Axmatova. očerk tvorčestva.* (Leningrad: Lenizdat, 1966).

Pjast [Pestovskij], Vladimir. *Vstreči.* (Moscow: Federacija, 1929).

Sajanov, V. *Ot klassikov k sovremennosti. Kritičeskie stat'i.* (Leningrad: Priboj, 1929).

Selivanovskij, Aleksej. *Očerki po istorii russkoj sovetskoj poèzii.* (Moscow: Xudožestvennaja literatura, 1936).

Struve, Gleb. *Russkaja literatura v izgnanii.* (New York: Chekhov Publishing House, 1956).

Txorževskij, Ivan. *Russkaja literatura.* (Paris: Vozroždenie, 1950).

Valentinov, N. [Vol'skij, Nikolaj]. *Two Years with the Symbolists.* Edited with a preface and notes by Gleb Struve. (Stanford University: The Hoover Institution on War, Revolution, and Peace, 1969).

Vinogradov, V. V. *O poèzii Anny Axmatovoj.* (Leningrad: 1925. Reprint The Hague: Mouton and Company, 1969).

Vladislavlev, I. V. [Gul'binskij, Ignatij Vladislavlevič]. *Russkie pisateli XIX–XX st.* (Moscow: Nauka, 1913).

Vojtolovskij, Lev Naumovič. *Očerki istorii russkoj literatury XIX–XX vekov. čast' vtoraja. Rešetnikov–Gor'kij.* (Moscow–Leningrad: State Publishing House, 1928).

Volkov, A. A. *Russkaja literatura XX veka. dooktjabr'skij period.* (Moscow: Prosveščenie, 1964).

Xodasevič, Vladislav. *Nekropol'. Vospominanija.* (Brussels: Les Éditions Petropolis, 1939).

Žirmunskij, Viktor. *Voprosy teorii literatury. (stat'i 1916–1926).* (Leningrad: 1928. Reprint 'S–Gravenhage: Mouton and Company, 1962).

ARTICLES IN RUSSIAN

Adamovič, Georgij. "Annenskij i Gumilev." *Novoe russkoe slovo.* (New York: May 2, 1965), p. 3.

_____. "Kommentarii." *Cex poètov,* No. 4 (Berlin: 1923), pp. 59-64.

_____. "Pamjati Annenskogo." *Cex poètov,* II-III (Berlin: 1922), pp. 92-97.

Aleksandrov, V. "Innokentij Annenskij." *Literaturnyj kritik,* nos. 5-6 (1939), pp. 115-134.

"Annenskij, Innokentij Fedorovič." *Malaja sovetskaja ènciklopedija.* Vol. I. (Moscow: 1930), col. 335.

Apollon, No. 3 (December, 1909), p. 48.

Arxippov, Evgenij. "Nikto i Ničej. Lirika Innokentija Annenskogo." *Mirtoryj venec.* (Moscow: Žatva, 1916), pp. 73-86.

Beskin, O. "Gumilev, Nikolaj Stepanovič." *Literaturnaja ènciklopedija.* Vol. III. (Moscow: Izdatel'stvo Kommunističeskoj Akademii, 1930. Ann Arbor: American Council of Learned Societies Reprints. Russian Series No. 20, J. W. Edwards, Edwards Bros., Inc., 1948), cols. 81-86.

Blagoj, D. "Annenskij, Innokentij Fedorovič." *Literaturnaja ènciklopedija.* Vol. I. (Moscow: Izdatel'stvo Kommunističeskoj Akademii, 1930. Ann Arbor: American Council of Learned Societies Reprints. Russian Series No. 20, J. W. Edwards, Edwards Bros., Inc., 1948), cols. 164-167.

Bobrov, Sergej. "Osip Mandel'štam. *Tristia." Pečat' i revoljucija,* No. 4 (April, 1923), pp. 259- 262.

Brjusov, Valerij. "Innokentij Annenskij. 'Kiparisovyj larec.' " *Russkaja mysl',* No. 6, pt. III (1910), pp. 162-163.

_____. "Iskusstvo i literatura RSFSR v èpoxu revoljucii (1917-1922). Včera, segodnja i zavtra russkoj poèzii." *Pečat' i revoljucija,* No. 7 (July, 1922), pp. 38-68.

_____. "Novye tečenija v russkoj poèzii. Akmeizm." *Russkaja mysl',* No. 3 (1913), pp. 124-133; No. 4 (1913), pp. 134-142; No. 8 (1913), pp. 71-80.

_____. "O 'reči rabskoj,' v zaščitu poèzii." *Apollon,* No. 9 (1910), pp. 31-34.

Buldeev, Aleksandr. "I. F. Annenskij kak poèt." *Žatva,* No. 3 (1912), pp. 195-219.

Burnakin, A. "Èstetičeskoe donkixotstvo." *Novoe vremja,* No. 12398 (September 7 [30], 1910), p. 4.

Čudovskij, Valerian. "Literaturnaja žizn'." *Russkaja xudožestvennaja letopis',* No. 20 (December, 1911), pp. 320-321.

Čukovskij, Kornej. "Axmatova i Majakovskij." *Dom iskusstv,* No. 1 (1921), pp. 23-42.

_____. "Innokentij Annenskij." *Reč',* No. 336 (December 7, 1909), p. 4.

_____. "Ob èstetičeskom nigilizme." *Vesy,* Nos. 3-4 (1906), pp. 79-81.

Čulkov, Georgij. "Zakatnyj zvon (I. Annenskij i Anna Axmatova)." *Otkliki.* Literatura. Iskusstvo. Nauka. (Supplement to newspaper *Den'),* No. 9 (1914), pp. 2-3.

Dolinin, A. "Akmeizm." *Zavety,* No. 5, Pt. 2 (May, 1913), pp. 153-162.

Dynnik, V. "Akmeisty." *Bol'šaja sovetskaja ènciklopedija.* Vol. I. (Moscow:

1929), cols. 823–824.

Evgen'ev, A. "Stixotvorenija Innokentija Annenskogo." *Literaturnoe obozrenie*, No. 14 (1939), pp. 31–35.

Fedorov, A. "Innokentij Annenskij." In *Stixotvorenija Innokentija Annenskogo*. (Leningrad: Sovetskij pisatel', 1939), pp. 3–30.

_____. "Notes." In Innokentij Annenskij, *Stixotvorenija i tragedii*. (Leningrad: Sovetskij pisatel', 1959), pp. 579–631.

_____. "Poètičeskoe tvorčestvo Innokentija Annenskogo." In Innokentij Annenskij. *Stixotvorenija i tragedii*. (Leningrad: Sovetskij pisatel', 1959), pp. 5–60.

Filippov, Boris. "Poèma bez geroja." In Anna Axmatova. *Sočinenija*. Edited by G. P. Struve and B. A. Filippov. Vol. II. (New York: Inter-Language Literary Associates, 1968), pp. 53–92.

Frank, Viktor. "Beg vremeni." In Anna Axmatova. *Sočinenija*. Edited by G. P. Struve and B. A. Filippov. Vol. II (New York: Inter-Language Literary Associates, 1968), pp. 39–52.

Ginzburg, L. Ja. "O prozaizmax v lirike Bloka." In *Blokovskij sbornik*. (Tartu: Tartuskij gosudarstvennyj universitet, 1964), pp. 157–171.

Gofman, Viktor. "Innokentij Annenskij. 'Kiparisovyj larec.'" *Novyj žurnal dlja vsex*, No. 21 (June, 1910), cols. 121–122.

_____. "Jazyk simvolistov." *Literaturnoe nasledstvo*. Vol. 27–28. (Moscow: Žurnal'no-gazetnoe ob"edinenie, 1937), pp. 54–105.

Gumileva, Anna. "Nikolaj Stepanovič Gumilev." *Novyj žurnal*, No. 46 (New York: 1956), pp. 107–126.

G. [urevič], L. [jubov']. "Pamjati I.F. Annenskogo." *Russkaja mysl'*, No. 1, pt. II (1910), pp. 163–166.

Ignatov, I. "Novye poèty. 'Akmeisty,' 'adamisty,' 'ègo-futuristy.'" *Russkie vedomosti*, No. 78 (April 4, 1913), p. 3; No. 80 (April 6, 1913), pp. 2–3.

Il'in, V. N. "Innokentij Annenskij i konec Periklova veka Rossii." *Vozroždenie*, No. 166 (Paris: October, 1965), pp. 42–59; No. 167 (Paris: November, 1965), pp. 37–50.

Ivanov, Georgij. "Introduction." In N. S. Gumilev, *Pis'ma o russkoj poèzii*. (Petrograd: Mysl', 1925), pp. 5–10.

Ivanov, Vjačeslav. "O poèzii I. F. Annenskogo." *Apollon*, No. 4 (January, 1910), pp. 16–24.

_____. "Zavety simvolizma." *Apollon*, No. 8 (1910), pp. 5–20.

Ivask, Ju. "Četyre kritika." *Novoe russkoe slovo* (New York: March 1, 1953), pp. 3, 8.

_____. "O poslevoennoj èmigrantskoj poèzii." *Novyj žurnal*, No. 23 (New York: 1950), pp. 195–214.

_____. "Slučevskij." *Novyj žurnal*, No. 79 (New York: June, 1965), pp. 270–284.

Jur'eva, Zoja. "Innokentij Annenskij o Gogole." *Novyj žurnal*, No. 45 (New York: June, 1956), pp. 136–148.

Karlinskij, Semen. "Veščestvennost' Annenskogo." *Novyj žurnal*, No. 85 (New York: December, 1966), pp. 69–79.

Krivič, Valentin. "Innokentij Annenskij po semejnym vospominanijam i rukopisnym materialam." *Literaturnaja mysl'*, No. 3 (1925), pp. 208–255.

"Kuzmin, Mixail Alekseevič." *Bol'šaja sovetskaja ènciklopedija*. Vol. XXXV (1st edition: Moscow: 1937), cols. 373–374.

Larin, Boris. "O 'Kiparisovom larce.'" *Literaturnaja mysl'*, No. 2 (1922–1923), pp. 149–158.

Levinson, Andrej. "Gumilev." *Sovremennye zapiski*, No. 9 (Paris: 1922), pp. 309–315.

Makovskij, Sergej. "Innokentij Annenskij–kritik." *Russkaja mysl'*, No. 1146 (Paris: December 12, 1957), p. 4; No. 1148 (Paris: December 17, 1957), p. 4; No. 1150 (Paris: December 21, 1957), p. 2.

————. "Nikolaj Gumilev po ličnym vospominanijam." *Novyj žurnal*, No. 77 (New York: 1964), pp. 157–189.

Malnina, E. "Innokentij Annenskij." *Literaturnyj sovremennik*, Nos. 6–7 (1940), pp. 210–213.

Margolin, Julij. "Pamjati Mandel'štama." *Vozdušnye puti*, No. 2 (New York: 1961), pp. 102–110.

Markov, Vladimir. "Mysli o russkom futurizme." *Novyj žurnal*, No. 38 (New York: 1954), pp. 169–181.

Mejer, Georgij. "Sergej Makovskij i Serebrjannyj vek." *Grani*, No. 54 (Frankfurt: 1963), pp. 208–217.

Močul'skij, K.[onstantin]. "Poètičeskoe tvorčestvo Anny Axmatovoj." *Russkaja mysl'*, Nos. 3–4 (Sofia: 1921), pp. 185–201.

Morozov, Al. "Mandel'štam, Osip Èmil'evič." *Kratkaja literaturnaja ènciklopedija*. Vol. IV. (Moscow: Sovetskaja ènciklopedija, 1967), cols. 568–570.

Muxin, Ar. "I. F. Annenskij (Nekrolog)." *Germes*, No. 20 (December 15, 1909), pp. 608–612.

Nedobrovo, N.V. "Anna Axmatova." *Russkaja mysl'*, No. 7, pt. II (1915), pp. 50–68.

Nikonov, V.A. "Annenskij, Innokentij Fedorovič." *Kratkaja literaturnaja ènciklopedija*. Vol. I. (Moscow: Sovetskaja ènciklopedija, 1962), col. 237.

Ocup, Nikolaj. "Nikolaj Stepanovič Gumilev." *Opyty*, No. 1 (New York: 1953), pp. 117–142.

Orlov, Vl. "Istorija odnoj 'družby-vraždy.'" In Aleksandr Blok and Andrej Belyj. *Perepiska*. (Moscow: 1940). Reprint Munich: Wilhelm Fink Verlag, 1969), pp. iv–lxiv.

Poljanskij, Valer'jan. "Social'nye korni russkoj poèzii ot simvolistov do našix dnej." In I. S. Ežov and E. I. Šamurin. *Russkaja poèzija XX veka*. (Moscow: 1925), pp. ix–xvii.

Punin, N. "Problema žizni v poèzii Annenskogo." *Apollon*, No. 10 (1914), pp. 47–50.

Red'ko, A. "U podnožija afrikanskogo idola." *Russkoe bogatstvo*, No. 6 (1913), pp. 317–332; No. 7 (1913), pp. 179–199.

Selivanovskij, A. "Očerki russkoj poèzii XX veka. glava vtoraja. Raspad akmeizma." *Literaturnaja učeba*, No. 8 (1934), pp. 22–36.

Setchkarev, V. M. "Gumilev dramaturg." In N. Gumilev. *Sobranie sočinenij v četyrex tomax*. Edited by G. P. Struve and B. A. Filippov. Vol. III. (Washington, D.C.: Victor Kamkin, Inc., 1966), pp. iii–xxxviii.

Sovsun, V. "Akmeizm ili Adamizm." *Literaturnaja ènciklopedija*. Vol. I. (Moscow: Izdatel'stvo Kommunističeskoj Akademii, 1930. Ann Arbor: American Council of Learned Societies Reprints. Russian Series No. 20, J. W. Edwards, Edwards Bros., Inc., 1948), cols. 70–73.

Struve, Gleb, publication and commentary. "Innokentij Annenskij i Gumilev. 'Neizvestnaja' stat'ja Annenskogo." *Novyj žurnal*, No. 78 (New York:

1964), pp. 279–287.

_____. "Iz arxiva N. S. Gumileva." *Opyty*, No. 1 (New York: 1953), pp. 181–190.

_____. "N. S. Gumilev. žizn' i ličnost'." In N. Gumilev. *Sobranie sočinenij v četyrex tomax.* Edited by G. P. Struve and B. A. Filippov. Vol. I. (Washington, D.C.: Victor Kamkin, Inc., 1962), pp. xii–xliv.

_____. "Notes." In N. Gumilev. *Sobranie sočinenij v četyrex tomax.* Edited by G. P. Struve and B. A. Filippov. Vol. IV. (Washington, D.C.: Victor Kamkin, Inc., 1966), pp. 529–634.

_____. "O. È. Mandel'štam. Opyt biografii i kritičeskogo kommentarija." In Osip Mandel'štam. *Sobranie sočinenij v trex tomax.* Edited by G. P. Struve and B. A. Filippov. Vol. I. (2nd edition Washington, D.C.: Inter-Language Literary Associates, 1967), pp. xxix–lxxxiv.

_____. "Pis'ma o russkoj poèzii." *Russkaja mysl'*, Nos. 6–7 (Prague: 1922), pp. 239–249.

_____. "Tri sud'by (Blok, Gumilev, Sologub)." *Novyj žurnal*, No. 16 (New York: 1947), pp. 209–228; No. 17 (New York: 1947), pp. 193–211.

_____. "Tvorčeskij put' Gumileva." In N. Gumilev. *Sobranie sočinenij v četyrex tomax.* Edited by G. P. Struve and B. A. Filippov. Vol. II. (Washington, D.C.: Victor Kamkin, Inc., 1964), pp. v–xl.

_____, and Filippov, B. A. Bibliography. In Anna Axmatova. *Sočinenija.* Edited by G. P. Struve and B. A. Filippov. Vol. II. (New York: Inter-Language Literary Associates, 1968), pp. 435–595.

_____, and Filippov, B. A. Bibliography. In Osip Mandel'štam. *Sobranie sočinenij v trex tomax.* Edited by G. P. Struve and B. A. Filippov. Vol. III. (New York: Inter-Language Literary Associates, 1969), pp. 415–542.

_____, and Filippov, B. A. Notes. In Osip Mandel'štam. *Sobranie sočinenij v dvux tomax.* Edited by G. P. Struve and B. A. Filippov. Vol. II. (New York: Inter-Language Literary Associates, 1966), pp. 515–626.

Struve, Nikita. "Vosem' časov s Annoj Axmatovoj." In Anna Axmatova. *Sočinenija.* Edited by G. P. Struve and B. A. Filippov. Vol. II. (New York: Inter-Language Literary Associates, 1968), pp. 323–346.

Šamurin, E.I. "Osnovnye tečenija v dorevoljucionnoj russkoj poèzii XX veka." In I. S. Ežov and E. I. Šamurin. *Russkaja poèzija XX veka.* (Moscow: 1925), pp. xviii–xxxv.

Taranovskij, K. "Pčely i osy v poèzii Mandel'štama: k voprosu o vlijanii Vjačeslava Ivanova na Mandel'štama." In the collection *To Honor Roman Jakobson. Essays on the Occasion of his 70th Birthday.* (The Hague: Mouton and Company, 1967), pp. 1973–1995.

Terapiano, Jurij. "Osip Mandel'štam." *Grani*, No. 50 (Frankfurt: 1961), pp. 102–122.

Tolstoj, Aleksej N. "N. Gumilev." *Poslednye novosti*, No. 467 (Paris: October 23, 1921), p. 2; No. 468 (Paris: October 25, 1921), p. 2.

Varneke, B. "I. F. Annenskij" [Nekrolog]. *Žurnal Ministerstva narodnogo prosveščenija*, No. 3 (1910), pp. 37–48.

_____. "Teatr Evripida." *Žurnal Ministerstva narodnogo prosveščenija*, No. 5 (1907), pp. 226–237.

Vejdle, V.V. "Peterburgskaja poètika." In N. Gumilev. *Sobranie sočinenij v četyrex tomax.* Edited by G. P. Struve and B. A. Filippov. Vol. IV. (Washington, D.C.: Victor Kamkin, Inc., 1968), pp. v–xxxvi.

Verxovskij, Jurij. "Put' poèta. O poèzii N. S. Gumileva." *Sovremennaja literatura.* (Leningrad: Mysl', 1925), pp. 93–143.

Vološin, M. "Liki tvorčestva, I. F. Annenskij–lirik." *Apollon,* No. 4 (January, 1910), pp. 11–16.

"Vstuplenie." *Apollon,* No. 1 (1910), pp. 3–4.

Xodasevič, Vladislav. "Ob Annenskom." *Èpopeja,* No. 3 (December, 1922), pp. 34–56.

Xolodnjak, I. "I. F. Annenskij. Teatr Evripida." *Žurnal Ministerstva narodnogo prosveščenija,* No. 7 (1909), pp. 86–89.

Zelinskij, F. "Evripid v perevode I. F. Annenskogo." *Pereval* (September, 1907), pp. 38–41; (October, 1907), pp. 40–46.

Žirmunskij, Viktor. "Preodolevšie simvolizm." *Russkaja mysl',* No. 12 (1916), pp. 25–56.

BOOKS IN LANGUAGES OTHER THAN RUSSIAN

Balakian, Anna. *The Symbolist Movement: A Critical Appraisal.* (New York: New York University Press, 1977).

Bazzarelli, Eridano. *La Poesia di Innokentij Annenskij.* (Milan: U. Mursia, 1965).

Bowra, C. M. *The Heritage of Symbolism.* (New York: Schocken Books, St. Martin's Press, 1961).

Bradbury, Malcolm and McFarlane, James, Editors. *Modernism.* (New York: Penguin Books, 1981).

Brereton, Geoffrey. *A Short History of French Literature.* (4th edition. Baltimore: Penguin Books, 1965).

Brown, Clarence. *The Prose of Osip Mandelstam.* (Princeton: Princeton University Press, 1965).

Chalsma, Howard William. *Russian Acmeism: Its History, Doctrine and Poetry.* (Seattle: University of Washington Dissertation, 1967).

Charvet, P. E. *A Literary History of France. Vol. V: The Nineteenth and Twentieth Centuries. 1870–1940.* (London: Ernest Benn Limited, 1967).

Cioran, Samuel. *Vladimir Solovyov and the Knighthead of the Divine Sofia* (Waterloo, Canada: Wilfrid Laurier Press, 1977).

Conrad, Barbara. *I. F. Annenskijs Poetische Reflexionen* (Munich: Wilhelm Fink Verlag: 1976).

Coulter, Catherine Nebolsine. *Aspects of the Poetry of Innokentij Annenskij.* (New York: Columbia University Master's Essay, 1966).

Donchin, Georgette. *The Influence of French Symbolism on Russian Poetry.* ('S-Gravenhage: Mouton and Company, 1958).

Erlich, Victor. *Russian Formalism. History–Doctrine.* (2nd edition. The Hague: Mouton and Company, 1965).

_____. *The Double Image: Concepts of the Poet in Slavic Literatures.* (Baltimore: The Johns Hopkins Press, 1964).

Harkins, William E. *Dictionary of Russian Literature.* (Paterson, New Jersey: Littlefield, Adams, and Company, 1959).

Holthusen, Johannes. *Russische Gegenwartsliteratur. I. 1890–1940. Die literarische Avantgarde.* (Bern and Munich: Francke Verlag, 1963).

_____. *Studien zur Åesthetik und Poetik des russischen Symbolismus.* (Göttingen: Vandenhoeck and Ruprecht, 1957).

_____, and Tschizewskij, Dmitrij. *Versdichtung der russischen Symbolisten.* (Wiesbaden: Otto Harrassowitz, 1959).

Ingold, Felix. *Innokentij Annenskij: Sein Beitrag zur Poetik des russischen Symbolismus* (Bern: Verlag Herbert Lang and Cie AG, 1970).

Kean, Beverly Whitney. *All the Empty Palaces* (New York: Universe Books, 1983).

Lo Gatto, Ettore. *Storia della Letteratura Russa.* (Florence: G.C. Sansoni, 1956).

Maline, Marie. *Nicolas Gumilev: Poète et Critique acméiste.* (Brussels: Palais des Académies, 1964).

Markov, Vladimir. *Russian Futurism: A History.* (Berkeley and Los Angeles: University of California Press, 1968).

_____, and Sparks, Merrill. *Modern Russian Poetry.* (Indianapolis, Kansas City, New York: The Bobbs–Merrill Company, Inc., 1967).

Mirsky, D. S. *A History of Russian Literature. II. After 1881.* Edited and abridged by Francis J. Whitfield. (New York: Alfred A. Knopf, 1949).

_____. *Modern Russian Literature.* (London: Oxford University Press, 1925).

_____. *Pushkin.* (New York: E.P. Dutton and Company, Inc., 1963).

Nebolsine, Arcadi. *Poshlost.* (New York: Columbia University Dissertation, 1971).

Obolensky, Dimitri, ed. *The Penguin Book of Russian Verse.* (Baltimore: Penguin Books, Inc., 1962).

Plato. *The Republic.* Translated by Francis MacDonald Cornford. (New York: Oxford University Press, 1957).

Poggioli, Renato. *The Poets of Russia, 1890–1930.* (Cambridge: Harvard University Press, 1960).

Pomorska, Krystyna. *Russian Formalist Theory and its Poetic Ambiance.* (The Hague: Mouton and Company, 1968).

Pozner, Vladimír. *Moderní Ruská Literatura. 1885–1932.* (Prague: Jan Laichter, Publishers, 1932).

_____. *Panorama de la Littérature Russe Contemporaine.* (Paris: Kra, 1929).

Rude, Jeanne, *Anna Akhmatova.* (Paris: Éditions Seghers, 1968).

Runes, Dagobert D., ed. *Dictionary of Philosophy* (Ames, Iowa: Littlefield, Adams and Company, 1960).

Runciman, Steven. *The Great Church in Captivity.* (Cambridge, England: Cambridge University Press, 1968).

Sampson, Earl Delos. *Studies in the Poetic Technique of Nikolaj Gumilev.* (Cambridge, Massachusetts: Harvard University Dissertation, 1968).

Schorske, Carl. *Fin–de–Siècle Vienna: Politics and Culture.* (New York: Alfred A. Knopf, 1980).

Setchkarev, Vsevolod. *Studies in the Life and Work of Innokentij Annenskij.* (The Hague: Mouton and Company, 1963).

Shapovaloff, Lubov Alex. *The Aesthetics and Poetics of Innokentij Annenskij.* (Seattle: University of Washington Dissertation, 1968).

Shattuck, Roger. *The Banquet Years: The Arts in France, 1885–1918.*

(Garden City, New York: Anchor Books, 1961).

Shaw,   J.   Thomas.   *The   Transliteration   of   Modern   Russian   for English–Language Publications.* (Madison: The University of Wisconsin Press, 1967).

Stavrou, Theofanis George, ed.   *Art and Culture in Nineteenth–Century Russia.* (Bloomington: Indiana University Press, 1983).

Strakhovsky, Leonid I.   *Craftsmen of the Word: Three Poets of Modern Russia.* (Cambridge, Massachusetts: Harvard University Press, 1949. 2nd edition Westbridge, Connecticut: Greenwood Press, 1969).

ARTICLES IN LANGUAGES OTHER THAN RUSSIAN

Brown, Clarence.   "Mandelshtam's Acmeist Manifesto.   Translated from the Russian with a Note. Osip Mandelshtam. 'The Morning of Acmeism.'" *The Russian Review*, Vol. 26, No. 1 (January–October, 1965), pp. 46–51.

Bukhshtab, Boris.   "The Poetry of Mandelstam."   *Russian Literature Triquarterly* (Fall, 1971), pp. 262–282.

Donchin, Georgette.   Introduction.   In Andrej Belyj.   *Vospominanija ob Aleksandre Bloke.*   (Letchworth, Hertfordshire, Great Britain: Bradda Books, Ltd., 1964), pp. 3–9.

Driver, Sam.   "Acmeism."   *The Slavic and East European Journal*, Vol. XII, No. 2 (1968), pp. 141–156.

_____.   "Anna Akhmatova: Early Love Poems." *Russian Literature Triquarterly* (Fall, 1971), pp. 297–325).

Fanger, Donald.   "On the Russianness of the Russian Nineteenth–Century Novel."   Theofanis George Stavrou, ed.   *Art   and   Culture   in Nineteenth–Century Russia.*   (Bloomington: Indiana University Press, 1983), pp. 40–56.

Ivask, George.   "Annenskij und Čechov." *Zeitschrift fur slavische Philologie*, XXVII (1959), pp. 136–148.

Kaun, Alexander.   "Russian Poetic Trends on the Eve of and the Morning After 1917."   *The Slavic Year Book* (American Series., I.   Being Vol. XX of *The Slavonic and East European Review* (1941), pp.   55–84.

Mickiewicz, Denis.   "*Apollo* and Modernist Poetics."   *Russian Literature Triquarterly* (Fall, 1971), pp. 226–261.

Muchnic, Helen.   "Three Inner Emigrés.   Anna Akhmatova, Osip Mandelshtam, Nikolai Zabolotsky." *The Russian Review*, Vol. 26 (January, 1967), pp. 13–25.

Nilsson, Nils Åke. "Osip Mandel'štam and his Poetry." *Scando–Slavica*, Vol. IX (1963), pp. 37–52.

Przybylski, Ryszard.   "Arkadia Osipa Mandelsztama." *Slavia Orientalis*, No. 3 (1964), pp. 243–262.

Rannit, Alexis.   "Anna Akhmatova Considered in a Context of Art Nouveau." In Anna Axmatova. *Sočinenija.* Edited by G.   P. Struve and B. A. Filippov.   Vol. II. (New York: Inter-Language Literary Associates, 1968), pp. 5–38.

Russell, Peter. "A Note on Osip Emilievitch Mandelshtam." *Delta* (January, 1959), pp. 1–11.

Sandomirsky, Vera. "The Forgotten Eve of the Revolution." *Poetry*, Vol. 26 (May, 1950), pp. 112–114.

Struve, Gleb. "Anna Akhmatova."   In Anna Axmatova. *Sočinenija.* Edited
    by G. P. Struve and B. A. Filippov.   Vol.   I.   (2nd edition New York:
    Inter–Language Literary Associates, 1967), pp.   5–16.

_____.   "Postscriptum for the Second Edition."   In Anna Axmatova.
    Sočinenija.   Edited by G. P. Struve and B. A. Filippov.   Vol. I.   (2nd
    edition New York: Inter–Language Literary Associates, 1967), pp. 16–18.

Terras, Victor. "Classical Motives in the Poetry of Mandel'štam."   *The Slavic
    and East European Journal*, Vol. X, No. 3 (1966), pp. 251–267.

Tucker, Janet G.   "Jurij Oleša's *Envy*: a Re–examination."   *The Slavic and
    East European Journal.* Vol. 26, No. 1 (Spring, 1982), pp. 56–62.

Whittaker, Robert T., Jr.   "Translator's Preface (Nikolai Gumilev and Acmeist
    Criticism)."   *Russian Literature Triquarterly* (Fall, 1971), pp. 139–140.

INDEX

Merežkovskij, Dmitrij, 11–12, 105, N6
Middle Ages, 83, 85, 87, 94–95
Močul'skij, Konstantin, 14
Modernism, and Mandel'štam, 95; and revolt, 11; in Russia, 9, 76–77. 97
Moscow, and Petersburg, and plastic arts 102; as "organically" Russian, 102
Mount Sinai, 112, N27
Music, and Blok, 105, N5; and Bugaev [Belyj], 105, N5; as ephemeral, 93; and
        Mandel'štam, 124, N77; and the Symbolists, 13, 105, N5
Mysticism, 82, 86, 93–94, 96, 124, N73, 128, N33

Narbut, Vladimir, 70, 80
Nature, as I. Annenskij's poetic theme, 47–48, 54
Nikolaj II, 18
Notre Dame, 83

Oblivion, as I. Annenskij's poetic theme, 29–30
"Obščestvo revnitelej xudožestvennogo slova," 70, 123, N58, 126, N9
Odysseus, 107–109, N43
Oleša, Jurij, 107, N36
Orthodox church, 40

Parnassians (French), 16, 19–20, 62, 71–72, 90, 109, N68, 109, N69, 120, N19,
        126, N14, 127, N15
Parny, Évariste-Désiré de, 88, 101
Persona, in I. Annenskij's verse, 48, 94; I. Annenskij and Axmatova, 94; in
        "Nocturno," 47; in "Stal'naja cikada," 45
Personification, in I. Annenskij's verse, 95–96
Petersburg, 102–104; and I. Annenskij, 103; and Mandel'štam, 102–104; and
        Moscow, 102; and Puškin, 103; and Russian culture, 102–103; as visual
        city, 102
Peter the Great, 22, 38; Falconet statue of, 37
Petrograd, 104
Petropolis, 103
Plastic arts, and I. Annenskij, 67; Moscow and Petersburg, 107, N33; and
        time, 93
Pluto, 103
Poet, in I. Annenskij's "Čelovek," 127–128, N27; in I. Annenskij's "Poèzija,"
        99; and architect, 94; and visual art, 94; as craftsman, 90, 93–94, 102;
        in Acmeism, 74; in Symbolism, 74; pose of, 123, N62; role of, 119, N15
Poetry, and language, 96; and nature, 116, N28; as center for Acmeists, 87; as
        craft, 90, 127, N15; as religion, 74; in I.   Annenskij's verse,   41;   in
        Gumilev's essay, 96; rational basis for, 96; separate from social criticism,
        116, N25
Poets, civic, 11; and critics, 65
Polyphemus, 107–108, N43
Positivist trends, and Nikolaj Annenskij, 108–109, N59
Potebnja, Aleksandr, 80
Prosaisms, and I. Annenskij's verse, 95, 128, N32
Proserpine, 103
Puškin, Aleksandr, and the Acmeists, 92–93, 97; and I. Annenskij, 17, 38, 65,
        92–93, 97, 100, 112, N22, 112, N26; and Axmatova, 88, 93, 100,111–112,
        N20; and art, 101; and Byronic hero, 93; civilization, spirit of, 97;
        Eugene Onegin, 92; and French culture, 101; and the Futurists, 15, 93;

OTHER SLAVICA BOOKS

American Contributions to the Eighth International Congress of Slavists (Zagreb and Ljubljana, Sept. 3-9, 1978), *Vol 1: Linguistics and Poetics,* ed. by Henrik Birnbaum, 1978; *Vol. 2: Literature,* ed. by Victor Terras, 1978

American Contributions to the Ninth International Congress of Slavists (Kiev 1983) *Vol. 1: Linguistics,* ed. by Michael S. Flier, 1983; *Vol. 2: Literature, Poetics, History,* ed. by Paul Debreczeny, 1983

Patricia M. Arant: *Russian for Reading,* 1981

Howard I. Aronson: *Georgian: A Reading Grammar,* 1982

James E. Augerot and Florin D. Popescu: *Modern Romanian,* 1983

John D. Basil: *The Mensheviks in the Revolution of 1917,* 1984

Henrik Birnbaum: *Lord Novgorod the Great Essays in the History and Culture of a Medieval City-State Part One: The Historical Background,* 1981

Henrik Birnbaum & Thomas Eekman, eds.: *Fiction and Drama in Eastern and Southeastern Europe: Evolution and Experiment in the Postwar Period,* 1980

Henrik Birnbaum and Peter T. Merrill: *Recent Advances in the Reconstruction of Common Slavic (1971-1982),* 1985

Karen L. Black, ed.: *A Biobibliographical Handbook of Bulgarian Authors,* 1982

Marianna Bogojavlensky: *Russian Review Grammar,* 1982

Rodica C. Boțoman, Donald E. Corbin, E. Garrison Walters: *Îmi Place Limba Română/A Romanian Reader,* 1982

Gary L. Browning: *Workbook to Russian Root List,* 1985

Catherine V. Chvany and Richard D. Brecht, eds.: *Morphosyntax in Slavic,* 1980

Jozef Cíger-Hronský: *Jozef Mak* (a novel), translated from Slovak by Andrew Cincura, Afterword by Peter Petro, 1985

Frederick Columbus: *Introductory Workbook in Historical Phonology,* 1974

Gary Cox: *Tyrant and Victim in Dostoevsky,* 1984

R. G. A. de Bray: *Guide to the South Slavonic Languages (Guide to the Slavonic Languages, Third Edition, Revised and Expanded, Part 1),* 1980

R. G. A. de Bray: *Guide to the West Slavonic Languages (Guide to the Slavonic Languages, Third Edition, Revised and Expanded, Part 2),* 1980

OTHER SLAVICA BOOKS

R. G. A. de Bray: *Guide to the East Slavonic Languages (Guide to the Slavonic Languages, Third Edition, Revised and Expanded, Part 3)*, 1980

Bruce L. Derwing and Tom M. S. Priestly: *Reading Rules for Russian: A Systematic Approach to Russian Spelling and Pronunciation, with Notes on Dialectal and Stylistic Variation*, 1980

Dorothy Disterheft: *The Syntactic Development of the Infinitive in Indo-European*, 1980

Thomas Eekman and Dean S. Worth, eds.: *Russian Poetics* Proceedings of the International Coloquium at UCLA, September 22-26, 1975, 1983

James Elliott: *Russian for Trade Negotiations with the USSR*, 1981

Michael S. Flier and Richard D. Brecht, eds.: *Issues in Russian Morphosyntax*, 1985

Michael S. Flier and Alan Timberlake, eds.: *The Scope of Slavic Aspect*, 1986

John M. Foley, ed.: *Oral Traditional Literature A Festschrift for Albert Bates Lord*, 1981

Diana Greene: *Insidious Intent: An Interpretation of Fedor Sologub's The Petty Demon*, 1986

Charles E. Gribble, ed.: *Medieval Slavic Texts, Vol. 1, Old and Middle Russian Texts*, 1973

Charles E. Gribble: *Russian Root List with a Sketch of Word Formation, Second Edition*, 1982

Charles E. Gribble: *A Short Dictionary of 18th-Century Russian/Словарик Русского Языка 18-го Века*, 1976

Charles E. Gribble, ed.: *Studies Presented to Professor Roman Jakobson by His Students*, 1968

George J. Gutsche and Lauren G. Leighton, eds.: *New Perspectives on Nineteenth-Century Russian Prose*, 1982

Morris Halle, ed.: *Roman Jakobson: What He Taught Us*, 1983

William S. Hamilton: *Introduction to Russian Phonology and Word Structure*, 1980

Pierre R. Hart: *G. R. Derzhavin: A Poet's Progress*, 1978

Michael Heim: *Contemporary Czech*, 1982

Michael Heim, Zlata Meyerstein, and Dean Worth: *Readings in Czech*, 1985

M. Hubenova & others: *A Course in Modern Bulgarian, Vols. 1 and 2*, 1983

Martin E. Huld: *Basic Albanian Etymologies*, 1984

OTHER SLAVICA BOOKS

Roman Jakobson, with the assistance of Kathy Santilli: *Brain and Language   Cerebral Hemispheres and Linguistic Structure in Mutual Light*, 1980

Donald K. Jarvis and Elena D. Lifshitz: *Viewpoints: A Listening and Conversation Course in Russian, Third Edition*, 1985; plus *Instructor's Manual*

Leslie A. Johnson: *The Experience of Time in Crime and Punishment*, 1985

Raina Katzarova-Kukudova and Kiril Djenev: *Bulgarian Folk Dances*, 1976

Emily R. Klenin: *Animacy in Russian: A New Interpretation*, 1983

Andrej Kodjak, Krystyna Pomorska, and Kiril Taranovsky, eds.: *Alexander Puškin Symposium II*, 1980

Andrej Kodjak, Krystyna Pomorska, Stephen Rudy, eds.: *Myth in Literature*, 1985

Andrej Kodjak: *Pushkin's I. P. Belkin*, 1979

Andrej Kodjak, Michael J. Connolly, Krystyna Pomorska, eds.: *Structural Analysis of Narrative Texts (Conference Papers)*, 1980

Demetrius J. Koubourlis, ed.: *Topics in Slavic Phonology*, 1974

Richard L. Leed, Alexander D. Nakhimovsky, and Alice S. Nakhimovsky: *Beginning Russian, Vol. 1*, 1981; *Vol. 2*, 1982; plus a Teacher's Manual

Edgar H. Lehrman: *A Handbook to Eighty-Six of Chekhov's Stories in Russian*, 1985

Lauren Leighton, ed.: *Studies in Honor of Xenia Gąsiorowska*, 1983

Rado L. Lencek: *The Structure and History of the Slovene Language*, 1982

Jules F. Levin and Peter D. Haikalis, with Anatole A. Forostenko: *Reading Modern Russian*, 1979

Maurice I. Levin: *Russian Declension and Conjugation: A Structural Description with Exercises*, 1978

Alexander Lipson: *A Russian Course, Parts 1, 2, and 3*, 1981; *Teacher's Manual* by Stephen J. Molinsky, 1981

Yvonne R. Lockwood: *Text and Context   Folksong in a Bosnian Muslim Village*, 1983

Sophia Lubensky & Donald K. Jarvis, eds.: *Teaching, Learning, Acquiring Russian*, 1984

Horace G. Lunt: *Fundamentals of Russian*, 1982

Paul Macura: *Russian-English Botanical Dictionary*, 1982

Thomas G. Magner, ed.: *Slavic Linguistics and Language Teaching*, 1976

OTHER SLAVICA BOOKS

Vladimir Markov and Dean S. Worth, eds.: *From Los Angeles to Kiev   Papers on the Occasion of the Ninth International Congress of Slavists,* 1983

Mateja Matejić and Dragan Milivojević: *An Anthology of Medieval Serbian Literature in English,* 1978

Peter J. Mayo: *The Morphology of Aspect in Seventeenth-Century Russian (Based on Texts of the Smutnoe Vremja),* 1985

Vasa D. Mihailovich and Mateja Matejic: *A Comprehensive Bibliography of Yugoslav Literature in English, 1593-1980,* 1984

Edward Możejko: *Yordan Yovkov,* 1984

Alexander D. Nakhimovsky and Richard L. Leed: *Advanced Russian,* 1980

The Comprehensive Russian Grammar of A. A. Barsov/ Обстоятельная грамматика А. А. Барсова, Critical Edition by Lawrence W. Newman, 1980

Felix J. Oinas: *Essays on Russian Folklore and Mythology,* 1985

Hongor Oulanoff: *The Prose Fiction of Veniamin Kaverin,* 1976

Slava Paperno, Alexander D. Nakhimovsky, Alice S. Nakhimovsky, and Richard L. Leed: *Intermediate Russian: The Twelve Chairs,* 1985

Papers for the V. Congress of Southeast European Studies (Belgrade, September 1984), ed. by Kot K. Shangriladze, 1984

Ruth L. Pearce: *Russian For Expository Prose, Vol. 1 Introductory Course,* 1983; *Vol. 2 Advanced Course,* 1983

Gerald Pirog: *Aleksandr Blok's* Итальянские Стихи *Confrontation and Disillusionment,* 1983

Stanley J. Rabinowitz: *Sologub's Literary Children: Keys to a Symbolist's Prose,* 1980

Gilbert C. Rappaport: *Grammatical Function and Syntactic Structure: The Adverbial Participle of Russian,* 1984

Lester A. Rice: *Hungarian Morphological Irregularities,* 1970

David F. Robinson: *Lithuanian Reverse Dictionary,* 1976

Robert A. Rothstein and Halina Rothstein: *Polish Scholarly Prose A Humanities and Social Sciences Reader,* 1981

Don K. Rowney & G. Edward Orchard, eds.: *Russian and Slavic History,* 1977

Catherine Rudin: *Aspects of Bulgarian Syntax: Complementizers and WH Constructions, 1986*

Ernest A. Scatton: *Bulgarian Phonology,* 1975 (reprint: 1983)

Ernest A. Scatton: *A Reference Grammar of Modern Bulgarian,* 1984

OTHER SLAVICA BOOKS

William R. Schmalstieg: *Introduction to Old Church Slavic, second edition, revised and expanded*, 1983

R. D. Schupbach: *Lexical Specialization in Russian*, 1984

Peter Seyffert: *Soviet Literary Structuralism: Background Debate Issues*, 1985

Michael Shapiro: *Aspects of Russian Morphology, A Semiotic Investigation*, 1969

J. Thomas Shaw: *Pushkin A Concordance to the Poetry*, 1985

Theofanis G. Stavrou and Peter R. Weisensel: *Russian Travelers to the Christian East from the Twelfth to the Twentieth Century*, 1985

Gerald Stone and Dean S. Worth, eds.: *The Formation of the Slavonic Literary Languages, Proceedings of a Conference Held in Memory of Robert Auty and Anne Pennington at Oxford 6-11 July 1981*, 1985

Roland Sussex and J. C. Eade, eds.: *Culture and Nationalism in Nineteenth-Century Eastern Europe*, 1985

Oscar E. Swan: *First Year Polish, second edition, revised and expanded*, 1983

Charles E. Townsend: *Continuing With Russian*, 1981

Charles E. Townsend: *Czech Through Russian*, 1981

Charles E. Townsend: *The Memoirs of Princess Natal'ja Borisovna Dolgorukaja*, 1977

Charles E. Townsend: *Russian Word Formation, corrected reprint*, 1975 (1980)

Walter N. Vickery, ed.: *Aleksandr Blok Centennial Conference*, 1984

Daniel C. Waugh, ed. *Essays in Honor of A. A. Zimin*, 1985

Daniel C. Waugh: *The Great Turkes Defiance On the History of the Apocryphal Correspondence of the Ottoman Sultan in its Muscovite and Russian Variants*, 1978

Susan Wobst: *Russian Readings and Grammatical Terminology*, 1978

James B. Woodward: *The Symbolic Art of Gogol: Essays on His Short Fiction*, 1982

Dean S. Worth: *Origins of Russian Grammar Notes on the state of Russian philology before the advent of printed grammars*, 1983

JOURNALS:

Folia Slavica

International Journal of Slavic Linguistics and Poetics

Oral Tradition